Beating the
Commodity Trap

Beating the Commodity Trap

How to Maximize Your Competitive Position
and Increase Your Pricing Power

Richard A. D'Aveni

HARVARD BUSINESS PRESS
BOSTON, MASSACHUSETTS

Library of Congress Cataloging-in-Publication Data

D'Aveni, Richard A.

   Beating the commodity trap : how to maximize your competitive position and increase your pricing power / Richard A. D'Aveni.

       p. cm.

       ISBN 978-1-4221-0315-9 (hardcover : alk. paper) 1.   Commercial products.
   2.   Consumption (Economics) 3.   Strategic planning. 4.   Competition.
   I.   Title.
       HF1040.7.D38 2009
       658.8'02—dc22

                                                                2009019394

To my wife, Veronika: The beauty of your soul,

the elegance of your manner, the intelligence of your mind,

and the kindness in your heart have convinced me

against all odds that there is perfection in this world.

Thank you for the inspiration.

CONTENTS

PREFACE

What do high-end fashion companies, New York restaurants, and Harley-Davidson have in common? Creeping commoditization. All are, or have been, in a battle against commoditization. Whether caused by a new low-cost competitor (such as fashion retailer Zara), new product innovation (such as enhanced customer experiences in restaurants), or the introduction of multiple substitutes and imitators (such as Honda, Suzuki, Victory, and Big Dog), price competition is always costly—and sometimes even deadly. It is clear that commoditization doesn't just happen to commodities.

My own interest in commoditization goes back to my 1994 book *Hypercompetition*. Some people were kind enough to say that this book changed the way people thought about strategy. The core idea was a new paradigm based on one theme: competitive advantages were becoming unsustainable because of globalization and technological disruption. That was in the mid-1990s. Since then I have watched and helped many business leaders cope with price wars and competition so fierce and furious that they wondered how they could survive, let alone prosper. Those experiences prompted me to write this book.

It seems to me that hypercompetition is more relevant now than when I first introduced the concept. Today many companies are facing hypercompetition on steroids! *Beating the Commodity Trap* is my attempt to help them understand and cope with those pressures.

My central argument is that many companies are in the grip of a particularly virulent form of hypercompetition. I call it the *commodity trap*, and it has the potential to destroy entire markets, disrupt whole industries, and drive previously successful firms out of business.

How does a firm get into a commodity trap in the first place? As tempting as it is to put the blame on cheap producers in China or some other external factor, most commodity traps are very much related to how managers act or do not act. In my experience, commoditization is usually the result of a failure to act early enough. Leaders do not see commoditization coming or fail to respond in a timely manner. Indeed, because many top managers are incentivized to focus on achieving short-term goals, they ignore longer-term trends such as the threat or onset of commoditization.

Why does this happen? Even if top management is familiar with some of the techniques I will be describing in this book, they are either uncomfortable using them or don't have the skill or experience to know when to use them. So, typically, they continue to fight against low-end competition by discounting their offerings. This has the unfortunate and unintended effect of increasing the depth and severity of the commodity trap. In a hole, executives often grab the nearest spade and carry on digging.

Nor is falling into the commodity trap simply the fault of the CEO or the board of directors. In fact, it is clear that commoditization is an increasingly important issue for all managers, including brand managers, product designers, and planners. What is needed is a new way of recognizing and responding to the threat of commoditization.

And that, in a nutshell, is the objective of *Beating the Commodity Trap*. The book provides a language for companies to identify and discuss the problems that they face and a framework to spot what most managers deny or what many ignore. The reality is that commoditization rarely simply happens to a firm. Most commoditization results when managers fail to innovate, issue bad products, or deny trends already in motion. After a while, firms are caught in the trap, and the dilemmas they created render them unable to get out of it. Commodity traps can be set by firms themselves or by their competitors.

COMMODITIZATION: WHAT TO DO?

The conventional wisdom for fighting commoditization advises either cost and capacity reduction (to avoid sacrificing margins) or continuous differentiation (to maintain a higher end position). But there is little evidence that these create long-term sustainable advantage. In fact, these may make the trap worse, trapping firms in never ending cycles of hypercompetition. Most managers do not know how to identify the root causes of commoditization so they are unable to avoid, eliminate, or in some cases, even use the causes to their advantage.

Over the last decade, I have developed a framework to help companies better understand the dynamics of price-product benefit positioning and to sharpen their own strategies for handling rampant commoditization. The three commodity traps framework is not simply a neat classroom theory—though it has been aired and debated in my classes. It offers strategies that have been proven to work in companies that have been caught up in fearsome price and proliferation wars.

To succeed over time, firms must manage commoditization by influencing the momentum, threats, and market power posed by rivals driving the different processes of commoditization. By improving their power over real prices, firms can actually beat their commodity trap rather than simply trying to outpace it.

But, to do so companies first have to understand what created the trap they are dealing with.

IDENTIFYING YOUR COMMODITY TRAP

Based on an in-depth study of more than thirty industries, *Beating the Commodity Trap* reveals the three most common patterns that create commodity traps: *deterioration, proliferation,* and *escalation.*

- *Deterioration:* Low-end firms enter with low-cost/low-benefit offerings that attract the mass market—as Zara did to high-end fashion companies in Europe.

- *Proliferation:* Companies develop new combinations of price paired with several unique benefits that attack part of an incumbents' market—as Japanese and American motorcycle makers did to Harley-Davidson.

- *Escalation:* Players offer more benefits for the same or lower price, squeezing everyone's margins—as Apple did with its series of iPods.

Analysis of the pattern of commoditization that is emerging and the language of deterioration, proliferation, and escalation can be a good starting point—the spark that ignites a vital discussion.

The book provides a tool for diagnosing the pattern of commoditization, your competitive position and shows how to improve it. This tool helps firms to increase their pricing power, by destroying the commoditization trap confronting you, escaping it, or even turning it to your advantage. It offers targeted strategies—beyond cost reduction or continuous differentiation—that companies have used to address these dilemmas successfully. Illustrated with a wealth of examples, this concise, practical guide gives you the framework and tactics you need to battle commoditization.

For each of the three traps, you will learn how to:

1. Identify the trap and whether it is the cause of commoditization in your market

2. Spot the trap before it damages your business

3. Escape the trap

4. Destroy the trap

5. Use the trap to your advantage

6. Choose which strategy is right for your situation

KEEPING YOUR TRAP SHUT

What I can say with assurance is that this framework and techniques are tried and true. They were developed and tested in real-life situations. My analysis of companies and their strategies and mistakes is frank and sometimes critical, but it is based on facts and hard data, rather than opinions and hand waving.

Some of the examples I use will be familiar. I make no apology for that. It is too easy sometimes to point at new and innovative companies as the exemplars of best practice. The snapshot is impressive, but roll the clock forward a couple of years and the picture is likely to change. I have deliberately preferred to take a longer-term view—since I am advocating strategies for the long-run, it makes sense to take a longitudinal view. My research looks at what has happened to a company over time. I have tried to consider not just the immediate impact of a strategy, but what happens next. And what happens after that.

If we needed any reminder of how the picture can change, then recent events have provided it in spades. While I was finishing this book, the business world was rocked by a number of shocks. From soaring oil prices (which then fell back) to bank bailouts, the financial turmoil has been immense. As I write, the United States is officially in a recession.

What does all this mean for companies caught in a commodity trap? The simple answer, of course, is that it makes this book more relevant and the strategies it describes more pressing than ever. A recession creates a particularly pernicious kind of commodity trap—

evaporation—which occurs when demand declines substantially. Evaporation reduces proliferation as firms cannot afford to produce or design product variety. But it encourages deterioration and escalation—as oversupply leads to lower prices. In a recession, customers become even more price sensitive, and may postpone purchases as they expect prices to decline. If demand evaporation gets out of hand then companies may be forced into a destructive cost-cutting cycle, with the accompanying pain. So most markets abandon escalation, and simply deteriorate. It is far better to act early to identify and tackle the cause of the commoditization trap.

But recessions don't last forever, and commoditization was virulent and pervasive even before the recession began. Therefore, this book is not intended solely for companies in recession. My purpose is to share the results of this decade-long effort to help managers avoid or escape their own commodity trap, regardless of whether it is occurring during good or bad times. I hope *Beating the Commodity Trap* will give you the frameworks and strategies to fight commoditization by recognizing the threats to your company's competitive positions and the opportunities to create new positions. Armed with these insights, you will be able to stake out an effective strategy to beat the commodity trap.

—Richard A. D'Aveni
Hanover, New Hampshire
August 2009

ONE

The Three Commodity Traps

From Diamonds to Glass

"**C**ommoditization" is an ugly word—and often an ugly reality—for companies around the world. From Wuhan to Washington, from Hannover, Germany, to Hanover, New Hampshire, commoditization is rife, a brutal fact of twenty-first century business life. Like the corporate equivalent of the black plague, almost every firm is suffering from commoditization in one form or another. In almost every industry, managers are being stunned as India and China exert their incredible economic potential, and technology continues to make major forward leaps. Timescales are shrinking and the commoditization clock is ticking.

"Everything commoditizes over time. The edges and points of difference get worn off by competition. The facets of diamonds are worn away and you are left with a piece of glass. It is easy to imitate and hard to innovate," Steve Heyer, the former CEO of Starwood Hotels & Resorts Worldwide and former COO of Coca-Cola, told me.[1] He's right. Everything becomes a commodity eventually. How to ensure that you emerge from the crucible of commoditization with diamonds is the subject of this book.

Merriam-Webster Online defines *commoditization* as "to render (a good or service) widely available and interchangeable with one provided by another company." Commoditization occurs when you have to constantly improve quality or other product benefits while decreasing prices to keep up with competitors. It also occurs if you have to lower product quality or other benefits to keep pace with falling prices. The problem is exacerbated when you are caught between rising input costs (such as energy, metals, and other raw materials) and a loss of pricing power for your products. Your costs increase but you simply cannot pass them onto your customers without killing your business. And commoditization occurs when demand evaporates, triggering round after round of price competition. Sound familiar?

If so, you are not alone. The impact of commoditization can be seen in industries as diverse as fast-moving consumer package goods and electronic products. Think of retailers such as Walmart and Tesco, which have introduced private-label products into their supermarkets, squeezing the margins of big-brand products and forcing companies, even giants like Unilever and Procter & Gamble, to rethink their strategies. Think of the impact that Dell once had on prices in the personal computer market. And now, of course, Dell itself faces further commoditization as low-cost producers from outside the United States enter its market.

Sometimes, too, the impact of commoditization in one part of a market can have a ripple effect throughout an entire industry. This is the case with Zara, the Spanish fashion retailer, which is directly disrupting both the low and middle segments of the fashion markets, with ripple effects that are even forcing changes in the high end of the market.

Private-label brands, the Dell effect, and "Zarafication" are all examples of what I call a *commodity trap*—where a company sees its competitive position being eroded so that it can no longer command a premium price in its market. In a commodity trap, consumers receive more product benefits for their money or pay lower prices for the same or lower levels of benefits. The result is that companies find that they can hold their prices and lose market share, or they can hold market share only by lowering prices. In either case, they have lost their pricing power. They experience squeezed profit margins whether input costs rise or remain stable. Over time, a company's product or service becomes indistinguishable from others in the market, and consumers buy on price alone—so a once-unique product becomes a commodity.

Of course, by now the Dell, Zara, and Walmart stories are all familiar. But familiarization should breed concern. In case you are under any illusions, let's be clear: commoditization can happen to any firm. Any product. Any time. And even if you don't see similarities between yourself and the more obvious examples, you're not necessarily safe—because not all commoditization is alike.

HARLEY-DAVIDSON: COMMODITIZATION OF A CLASSIC

If you are not yet convinced, consider Harley-Davidson. The ultimate premium-priced, iconic product surely defies commoditization. In a world where products routinely turn to glass, Harley has been a perpetual commercial diamond. At least, that's what you might think. But let's dig deeper and try to understand this classic corporate case in commoditization terms.

Prem de la Prem

Despite its cult status, Harley-Davidson has had to survive several rounds of tough price-benefit competition. What should have been a long, straight highway has had a few hidden dips—and in these commoditization has lurked, whether in the guise of cheaper Japanese competitors like Honda or sexy upstarts at the top end of the market like Big Dog.

Founded in 1903, Harley-Davidson came to define the motorcycle industry in the United States. But in the 1970s, it encountered its first major commoditization trap. The company was undermined by a reputation for poor quality, lack of innovation, and poor customer service. Japanese rivals such as Honda, Suzuki, and Yamaha took advantage of this weakness to offer motorcycles at lower prices with better reliability.

As these rivals offered greater benefits at lower prices, the outcome was predictable, if not inevitable. In spite of its legendary status, Harley's market share shrank from 39 to 23 percent between 1979 and 1983. Harley-Davidson was truly caught in a commodity trap. The question facing the company's senior managers was what to do about it. The company could either slash prices to hold on to its market share or hold prices but concede share. But neither move would lead to financial health, given the firm's fixed-cost structure. And each would only lead to an intensification of price-product benefit competition.

The Road Back

Harley's future looked grim. But after a leveraged management buyout in 1981, Harley's leadership turned the company around. The way out of the trap was to revisit customer benefits. While keeping its classical advantage in engine power, the company emphasized a valuable secondary benefit to its products: branding based on its "rebel" image and iconic status. This made the Japanese rivals' reliability advantage less important as a factor in purchasing and valuing motorcycles. Rebels care more for role models than reliability.

Key to this turnaround was the launch in 1983 of the Harley Owners Group (HOG). HOG became the world's largest factory-sponsored motorcycle club and now has over one million members worldwide. HOG helped Harley sell an array of branded apparel and collectibles, further encouraging its adventurous Harley lifestyle and bad-boy image. If you couldn't afford a Harley, you could always buy a Harley jacket or Harley emblem. The company roared back in the late 1980s. In 2003, its centennial year, the company announced record revenues of $4.6 billion, up 13 percent from the previous

FIGURE 1-1

Harley takes the high road

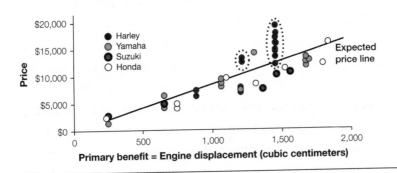

year.[2] Harley was back on the highway, and commoditization was, it seemed, an oil slick in the rear-view mirror.

Consider the very simple price-benefit map shown in figure 1-1.[3] My analysis found that, in 2002, "hog-wild" customers were willing to pay an average 38 percent premium for a Harley-Davidson motorcycle, over a similarly equipped motorcycle from one of the big four Japanese companies (Honda, Yamaha, Kawasaki, and Suzuki)—despite the fact that Japanese models offered 8 to 12 percent more power for the same price, based on engine displacement. Harley customers were willing to pay a third more for a tenth *less* power. In fact, Harley's image was so powerful that it even became the dominant brand in large-displacement motorcycles *in Japan*.

The feeling of victory was understandable. Harley's turnaround shows how a company can (initially, at least) successfully fight back against commoditization by differentiating its products.

Trouble in Hog Heaven

But that's only part of the story. Another commoditization trap loomed: the big hog was about to meet the Big Dog.

As Harley celebrated its victory over its Japanese rivals, two new U.S. motorcycle brands were making their marks on the industry: Victory (owned by snowmobile developer Polaris Industries) and

Big Dog. By 2004, while it was not evident that Harley was losing its grip on the market, deeper analysis showed Harley's brand was no longer automatically top hog. In 2004, my researchers and I calculated the advantage of Harley's brand compared with other companies by quantifying how much higher Harley's prices were than expected prices for bikes of similar displacement, accessories, and features.

Our price-benefit analysis of the 2004 market revealed an emerging challenge to Harley's price-benefit positioning.[4] It showed that Harley did not earn a premium over its new U.S. competitors. In fact, Victory and Big Dog's highly customized motorcycles commanded a 41 percent premium *over* Harley-Davidson for the same engine, features, and accessories.

From a strategic perspective, this suggested that Harley-Davidson's brand was still potent enough to keep the Japanese manufacturers at bay, but was at a disadvantage when it came to U.S.-made rivals. Both these rivals have remained fairly small in terms of sales volume. Big Dog, for example, produced just 25,000 motorcycles between starting life in 1994 and 2009 (while Harley routinely shipped over 300,000 motorcycles annually). But, the all-American threat was already becoming clear in 2004 and is now a reality. Along the way, Big Dog became the world's largest manufacturer of custom motorcycles. And Harley found itself fending off both lower-priced Japanese competition *and* premium American manufacturers.

Let's look at this situation more closely. Harley was leaving money on the table compared with its American rivals because its services, level of customization, and image were not as good as theirs. Harley's macho, bad-boy image did not appeal to Generation X and Y consumers—and women. By 2007, American women were the fastest-growing segment of the U.S. motorcycle market, purchasing more than 100,000 motorcycles per year.[5] According to the Motorcycle Industry Council, women now number over 12 percent of riders, up 29 percent since 2003.[6]

While women accounted for 12 percent of Harley's sales, spending about $300 million, not counting clothing and other accessories, the company lagged behind rivals such as Kawasaki and Suzuki in reaching this growing segment, in part because these Japanese competitors offer smaller, less intimidating bikes. So Harley was getting caught in a trap set by proliferating products that surrounded its core market.

Both Generation X and Y consumers saw Harley as their father's motorcycle—think GM and Oldsmobile. The average Harley rider is a married man in his forties with an income of $84,300.[7] An article in *Marketing Trends* noted how some observers felt that Harley had "lost its cool" and rivals such as Big Dog had donned the leather jacket of cooldom.[8] The new rivals capitalized on the desire for a new image—the "New American Bike"—in contrast to Harley's traditional Hell's Angel–open highway–leather jacket and shades–*Easy Rider* image. Victory and Big Dog's highly customized products were trumping Harley-Davidson's rebel image by changing motorcycle riding from an act of machismo to one of individualism and self-expression.

The Commodity Skid

Industry experts were astounded when I showed them these results suggesting that Harley was on the edge of another commodity trap in 2004. They didn't agree and insisted that Harley would remain dominant.

The most readily available confirmation of this dominance is market share data. Of course, current market share is not a predictor of a company's ability to charge premium prices (think General Motors again). Actually, at the same time as the industry insiders dismissed my take on their market, Harley dealers were engaged in extensive price discounting to keep sales up. More important, the analysis provided an early warning of Harley's 2005 stock price slide and gave hard data about the creeping commodity trap suggesting the need to protect, modify, and refresh its brand image.

Because these insiders were using traditional strategic analysis such as measuring market share, the threat was simply not apparent. Harley still had the largest share of the market (just under 50 percent), but the fact that its dealers were discounting to keep sales up disguised the problem. They were, in essence, buying market share with lower prices.

Yet it wasn't until 2006—fully two years after my analysis identified the problem—that the company responded, introducing a range of initiatives to support its strategy to attract new customers. In particular, it hoped its Buell brand would appeal to younger riders and women.

The reality is that Buell has not yet made a big difference to Harley's financial performance. In fact, although Harley's stock price rose in mid-2007 (and only in response to rumors that it might be taken over by Honda), it fell again after dealers indicated sales volumes would be weaker than expected. Harley shipped 303,000 bikes in 2008, compared with 331,000 in 2007. (As I write, sales of 264,000 to 273,000 are anticipated for 2009.)

Now, I am not saying I am amazingly prescient. But through price-product benefit analysis I was able to spot the signs of creeping commoditization. Think about it. Where would Harley be now if it had acted two years earlier? Think about your own company. Do you know what's happening in your market? Are you sure? Are the trends you see just recessionary, or will you see commoditization even as the inevitable recovery occurs?

WHY DIFFERENTIATION IS NOT ENOUGH

If it can happen to top-end fashion companies, creeping commoditization can happen to you. Experience shows that differentiation is not enough. Soon everyone else has the same bells and whistles. What use is a new fashion collection when it can be speedily and cheaply imitated by Zara?

Harley's experience is all the more chastening because it appeared to have escaped the trap. Faced with imitation and the proliferation of Japanese and American rivals—Japanese manufacturers even attempted to imitate Harley's signature "rolling thunder" sound— Harley found ways to separate itself from the pack through focusing on brand image. The strategy was successful at first, but the escape from commoditization is an ongoing process of managing the price-benefit equation. While Harley successfully differentiated itself from Japanese rivals, it faced new competition from American rivals offering different benefits that earned higher prices by appealing to changes in the consumer base. Now, Harley is caught between lower-priced Japanese bikes and higher-priced American customized bikes. Not an enviable position for the long term, especially as demand continues to evaporate.

The fact is, product-based advantages are narrowing and fleeting, making it harder for companies to extract a price premium in most markets. Just about every manager I talk to is engaged in differentiation. But very few of them feel that continuous differentiation is a solution. They simply don't get the results they expect. Why? Because everyone else is doing it, too. In the end they feel like the Red Queen in *Alice in Wonderland*, who noted that: "Here you must run faster and faster to get nowhere at all!" Managers are no strangers to running on the same spot. Many conclude they need to get better at continuous differentiation by infusing greater customer orientation into their organizations. But, once again, everyone else is doing this as well.

Too many people see the race for differentiation like the old joke about two friends confronted by a bear in the woods. One friend puts on his running shoes. The other points out that he can't hope to outrun the bear. The first friend responds: "I know, but all I have to do is outrun you!" But avoiding a commodity trap is different: unlike a simple race of the swift, in commoditization, the bear often wins, getting *both* competitors, or the race goes not to the swift but to the person *running in the right direction*. Differentiation can be a powerful way to change positioning. But it is only part of the solution to the commodity trap. To run in the right direction, you have to understand how commoditization occurs. You have to be able to recognize the different traps and know how to beat them. This means that firms must not just differentiate their products, but must also use differentiation to change their industries' structures in ways that mitigate, moot, or eliminate the different traps. Identifying these traps and showing how to get out of them is the focus of this book.

THE THREE COMMODITY TRAPS

In a hypercompetitive environment, the dynamics of price-benefit maneuvering have become more intense, rapid, and significant. There are a lot of bears out there! The Walmart effect, the rise of China, offshoring and outsourcing to low-cost countries, recession, eroding consumer loyalty, discontinuous technological revolutions, and other relentless forces of hypercompetition are eroding and unseating the price and benefit positions of leading products in almost every market.[9] The spread of Six Sigma, Total Quality Management (TQM), customer relationship management (CRM), and supply chain management (SCM) software and new manufacturing technologies is leveling the global playing field and erasing cost and product benefit-based advantages.

In industry after industry, the confluence of these factors is creating an inevitable—arguably unstoppable—pressure toward commoditization. It was this phenomenon that I set out to explore with my team of researchers. I wanted to understand: first, the competitive mechanisms that lead markets to commoditize over time; second, how the commoditization actions of one firm affect their rivals; and finally, and most crucially, whether there were ways to reverse or evade the commoditization forces and escape from or destroy the commodity trap (see figure 1-2).

My team and I studied companies in more than thirty industries—from restaurants to retailing, from watches to watching the news, from

FIGURE 1-2

The three commodity traps framework

	Deterioration ↓ Price ↓ Benefits to customers	Proliferation ↓↑ Price ↓↑ Benefits	Escalation ↓ Price ↑ Benefits
Description **The causes**	*Chapter 2*: Caused by a firm with a dominant low cost–low benefit position that swallows market share and upsets the positioning of those around it.	*Chapter 3*: Caused by multiple threats due to substitutes, imitators, market fragmentation, and new-product innovation. Opens many new price-benefit positions, surrounding and eroding the firm's product uniqueness.	*Chapter 4*: Caused by rising benefits for the same or lower price. Rivals jockey to offer more value to customers driving competition down toward the lower right-hand corner of the price-benefit map.
Dilemmas **The challenges**	You can't beat 'em, but if you run away from them, you have to abandon the segments that you do best, so either way profits will erode.	You can't fight everyone everywhere, all the time. But if you don't, you are stung to death by a swarm of bees.	Price-benefit competition can be costly, but no company can afford to be the first to blink and end the game of one-upmanship.

amateur photography to advanced materials, from turbines to tires, from automobiles to artificial sweeteners, from music-playing devices to motorcycles, and from making ships to making chips. We quantified, verified, and expanded on the commoditization patterns identified from my consulting and action-research.

To understand the ways commodity traps develop, I asked fundamental questions:

- What are the common patterns of commoditization?

- Is commoditization a different process for every industry or possibly even for every firm and industry?

I then sought answers by asking:

- What is the underlying competitive movement or flow of prices and benefits in this industry and how is it changing the price-benefit analysis?

- Given these patterns of commoditization, how are companies finding a way out?

Using these questions, I identified the three most common patterns that created commodity traps and found that the descent into commodity hell was neither inevitable nor incontrovertible. By identifying the dilemmas these commodity traps presented, I was able to understand the strategies—beyond continuous differentiation—that companies have used to address these dilemmas successfully.

I have found that commodity traps occur for three primary reasons:

- *Deterioration:* First, I found a number of industries suffering from the emergence of a dominant low-end competitor, such as Zara, whose imitations of designer products caused the "Zarafication" of the European fashion market. This type of commoditization occurs when a low-end firm offers a value proposition that is so superior in the eyes of customers that others are left in the dust. Typically, these are very low cost–low benefit products or services that attract the mass market, such as Walmart's "every day low prices" approach to merchandising. In the United States, no manufacturer went after the low end of the motorcycle market. In India, however, Bajaj's low-priced, low-power motorbikes captured a large part of the two-wheeler market for decades, as did Honda's Cub in Japan. The emergence of such a low-end competitor—for example, at the time of writing, the impending development of a $2,000 car in India and a $6,000 version for the United States—poses a serious challenge to incumbents in the car and motorcycle industries because established firms have cultural, cost-structure, and labor cost differences, often finding it difficult to compete with the challenger on their own terms. This leads to the deterioration of both prices and benefits.

    In the deterioration trap, prices go down; and benefits go down, too.

- *Proliferation:* Second, I found many industries suffering from product proliferation. The motorcycle market is a case in point. Companies develop new value propositions—new combinations of price and several unique benefits—that attack part of an incumbents' market. The Japanese motorcycle makers did this in the 1990s by creating a series of bikes for thrill seekers (sport and racing bikes), responsible adventurers (travelers and vacationers) and commuters (basic transportation), siphoning off customers who did not really fit Harley's motorcycle gang and weekend rebel segments, and partially commoditizing other Harley products by offering alternatives that overlapped with Harley's main benefits. Meanwhile, the American rivals—Big Dog and Victory—appealed to niches surrounding Harley's position.

In the proliferation trap, prices go up or down, while benefits go up or down in all directions around a focal firm's products.

- *Escalation:* Third, I found industries, such as consumer electronics, in which prices were declining while benefits were increasing. The value that a product offers to customers can quickly get out of whack with the market. In other words, the market witnesses an escalation in the ratio of benefits offered by the product to prices charged. So companies offer more for the same or lower price. This is what Apple did in iPods, reducing prices while improving functionality and outflanking the entire lines of other branded producers of digital music devices. This leads to a situation where price is constantly driven down even as product benefits continue to rise, squeezing margins. We see this frequently in markets where technology is advancing rapidly, but can occur in many other markets as well.

In the escalation trap, prices go down; and benefits go up.

Any one of these three patterns can lead to complete commoditization of a product market, a point where a firm's product margins and/or market share are rapidly, if not completely, disappearing. To help you identify which commodity traps are operating in your firm's markets, see "The Commodity Trap Checklist," which summarizes the three traps and the strategic dilemmas they create for managers.

The Commodity Trap Checklist

Which of these three traps are threatening your firm's markets? Consider the following questions:

Deterioration

- Has a dominant low-cost competitor emerged in your market, disrupting the status quo?

- Do economies of scale make it impossible for you to compete with some rivals on price?

- Are customers less and less willing to pay for additional benefits such as service and industry expertise?

- Are your margins falling, and are you losing market share despite the fact that you are lowering prices to match the competition?

Proliferation

- Is your market increasingly fragmented, with new offerings and variations introduced all the time?

- Is your main product's value proposition being undermined by new offerings targeted at ever narrower market niches?

- Are you frustrated by insufficient resources to fight marketing and innovation wars on too many fronts surrounding your main product?

- Are you under constant pressure to reduce your prices just to retain your existing customers because rivals have surrounded you on all sides?

Escalation

- Do you feel like you are locked into an arms race with competitors, constantly adding new features and benefits and lowering prices just to keep up?

- Do you find that one competitor is making money by leading the escalation of benefits and lowering of prices, while you are trapped in a game of nonprofitable catch-up?

- Do you find that the primary benefit that excited customers yesterday is taken for granted today and will be no more than entry stakes for tomorrow?

- Do your customers have the power to constantly demand more for less money?

THE RIGHT STRATEGY TO FIT THE TRAP

Once a company is caught in a commodity trap, differentiation is rarely enough to get it back out. Indeed, the reason most companies find themselves in the trap in the first place is because they failed to innovate early enough to avoid it or they later differentiated and cut prices so much that they have exacerbated the trap. So, if differentiation alone is not sufficient to beat the commodity traps, what can companies do?

To be successful in the long run, you must indentify and resolve the dilemmas and challenges created by *each* particular trap. Figure 1-3 summarizes how to identify each trap and lists some of the most frequent solutions to each.

While figure 1-3 illustrates the common patterns and different solutions that I have found across industries, there are many variations on these three themes. Every company and industry faces distinctive challenges in price-benefit maneuvering that require careful analysis using price-benefit analysis—the mapping of price versus product benefits to look for trends and statistical relationships between price

FIGURE 1-3

Strategies for beating the three commodity traps

	Deterioration ↓ Price ↓ Benefits to customers	Proliferation ↓↑ Price ↓↑ Benefits	Escalation ↓ Price ↑ Benefits
Symptoms **How to identify**	• Low-cost player disrupting status quo • Economies of scale favor the competition • Customers less willing to pay for expertise and superior service • Margin and share falling—despite price cuts	• Market fragmenting with new offerings • Rivals targeting narrowing niches • Inability to fight on all fronts • Pressure to cut prices just to keep existing customers	• Caught up in an arms race • Constantly playing catch-up • Yesterday's competitive advantage is today's entry stakes • Customers demanding more for less (high buyer power)
Solutions **The strategies**	Managing market power To reduce, use, or avoid the power of the low-end discounter	Managing threats To reduce the magnitude and number of threats faced, to conserve resources, or to build capability to fight a multifronted war	Managing momentum To control the movement of products toward the low price–high benefit corner of the price-benefit map
Escape the trap	*Sidestep* the low-end player's market power	*Select* your threats (narrow the fronts)	*Re-seize* the momentum
Destroy the trap	*Undermine* the low-end player's market power	*Overwhelm* the threats	*Reverse* the momentum
Turn the trap to your advantage	*Contain* the low-end player's market power to the low end	*Outflank* (outproliferate) the threats	*Harness* the momentum

and product benefits. There are also short-term opportunities that can emerge within these broader patterns; these require strategic adjustments. That's why I have spent the last ten years developing this framework and price-benefit mapping tools to help managers identify and beat their commodity traps. The rest of the book demonstrates how these commodity traps work in practice, and describes the strategies for beating them—*escaping the trap, destroying the trap*, or *take advantaging of the trap* to use it as bait that lures rivals in, while you get out.

Chapter 2 outlines practical strategies for beating the deterioration trap. Using real-life examples, it explains how you can spot the deterioration spiral before it takes hold of your business and destroys it. It explains why even high price–high quality players are affected by ripple effects at the low end of the market and how the market power of the low-end player is the underlying problem that must be dealt with using *market power management strategies.*

Chapter 3 describes the proliferation commodity trap, and explains how you can identify the telltale signs early on so that you can take evasive action. It examines the options for dealing with the dilemmas caused by fighting numerous threats, using what I have labeled as *threat-management strategies.* Using real examples of how companies have sidestepped the proliferation trap—or taken control to turn proliferation against their rivals—the chapter explains how to beat this potentially debilitating trap.

Chapter 4 examines the escalation trap. It explains how you can identify when you are caught in this trap and outlines practical responses that will turn the situation to your advantage or destroy the trap. The chapter discusses how escalation results from the seemingly unstoppable momentum created by constant one-upmanship as rivals offer more benefits at lower prices. The chapter explains how you can use strategies to "manage the momentum."

Finally, having demonstrated how you can beat the commodity traps, in chapter 5 I offer some insights on the next wave of competitive pressures. In particular, this chapter considers the impact of ongoing disruption and price pressure and how companies can confront them. These tools and strategies are akin to using a strategic global positioning system (GPS), allowing companies to pinpoint where they are on the competitive map and what they have to do to reach new coordinates. These insights and tools are especially valuable for dealing with disruptive technologies, new business models, and aggressive hypercompetition.

My research suggests that most managers can feel when there is something wrong, but cannot articulate why they are trapped. They aren't blind, but they are often stunned because they can't find a way out of the dilemma trapping them. I hope this book offers a language to describe their situation and a practical set of actions that will set them free—and help them avoid traps in the future.

So welcome to a new world full of commodity traps and ways to beat them. These traps will offer many challenges, but it is best to focus on the opportunities created by commoditization. After all, the best golf courses are the ones with numerous sand traps and other obstacles that offer the enjoyment of overcoming them. The traps are what make us stronger competitors when we learn to escape, undermine, or turn them to our advantage.

TWO

The Deterioration Trap

How to Manage Market Power to Beat Low-End Competitors

Sometimes research has an accidental quality. I was reminded of this recently when I bought a Louis Vuitton handbag for my daughter. She was very pleased until she took it to school and her classmates made fun of her for buying a knockoff. I knew it was a genuine Louis Vuitton—and had the bill to prove it! But her peers could not tell, and that was actually more important.

The quality of imitators, private labels, and generic products has increased to the point where even discerning eyes—and, believe me, teenage girls are *very* discerning—have a hard time telling the difference. The handbag episode encouraged me to look further afield. I looked at the discount racks of T.J. Maxx and found Armani suits. I found Burberry at BJ's Wholesale Club. And these weren't last year's fashions. Big-name fashion brand goods can now be found in such stores during the same season they are launched.

It is a familiar story. The fashion industry once had a clear price-benefit line. Premium designers charged top dollar. Now, the industry is being transformed, and valuable brands find themselves increasingly commoditized.

There's more. Knockoffs and discounting among premium brands are a symptom of broader changes. One of the biggest challenges is emerging at the low end of the European fashion market where the Spanish retailer Zara, owned by Inditex, is using new mass production processes and sourcing strategies to offer low-priced imitations of newly released designer products.[1]

The emergence of Zara and other fashion-forward discounters is leading to a low-end migration of buyers in the European women's fashion market.[2] This is affecting the entire market. First the lower (mass-market) and mid-price-point segments are affected as direct competitors. But as the middle-price-point brands change their strategies, the ripples have spread to the very top designers, forcing everyone in the industry to shape a response.

Zarafication is not unusual but it is always impressive. It is an exemplar of the first common commodity trap: deterioration (see figure 2-1).

FIGURE 2-1

Chapter 2 summary: The deterioration trap

	Deterioration ↓ Price ↑ Benefits to Customers
Description The causes	Caused by a firm with a dominant low cost–low benefit position that swallows market share and upsets the positioning of those around it
Dilemmas The challenges	You can't beat 'em, but if you run away from them, you have to abandon the segments that you do best, so either way profits will erode.
Symptoms How to identify	• Low-cost player disrupting status quo • Economies of scale favor the competition • Customers less willing to pay for expertise and superior service • Margin and share falling—despite price cuts
Solutions The strategies	**Managing market power** To reduce, use, or avoid the power of the low-end discounter
Escape the trap	*Sidestep* the low-end player's market power.
Destroy the trap	*Undermine* the low-end player's market power.
Turn the trap to your advantage	*Contain* the low-end player's market power to the low end.

Deterioration occurs when a low-end competitor creates a dominant low price–low benefit position that expands the market share at the low end. Deterioration is created by declining price and lowering (or consistently low) positioning on the product's primary benefit—the most important benefit offered by products in the industry. Like a black hole, the low-end competitor creates such a dominant price-benefit position that it literally swallows up positions around it. We have seen this pattern with the emergence of value retailers such as Walmart and no-frills airlines such as Southwest or Ryanair. These competitors are such a force to be reckoned with that everyone else has to compete on their terms.

TELLTALE SIGNS

The arrival of a dominant low-end player shakes up the market power of the industry, as Southwest did in the airline industry, Dell once did in computers, or Walmart is still doing in retailing. It is very hard for incumbents to compete with these disruptive players using their existing cost structures. Responses to deterioration must address the shift in market power and manage its distribution across the industry. Firms can do this by adopting market power management strategies that moot, contain, or undermine the market power of the low-end discounters causing the market deterioration. But first they have to recognize what is happening in their market.

So, what are the telltale signs of deterioration? If the following sound familiar, then you are likely to be facing this trap:

- A dominant low-cost competitor has emerged in your market, disrupting the status quo.

- The economies of scale enjoyed by the disrupting company make it impossible for you to compete on price.

- Customers are less and less willing to pay for additional benefits such as superior service and industry expertise.

- Your margins are falling and you are losing market share, even though you have lowered prices and product benefits to catch up with the competition.

The rest of this chapter examines how deterioration occurs and the most effective strategies to combat it.

FASHIONING BRIDGES

To better understand the phenomenon of deterioration, let's look a little deeper into the fashion industry. What Zara is doing is simply the latest disruptive move in an industry in which business models are constantly being innovated. To fully understand the world of fashion, we need to go back to the 1960s when French and Italian haute couture fashion houses transformed what was a local boutique industry into a global market. Fashion houses typically hand-produced one- or two-of-a-kind products personally designed by a brilliant artist as a special order for wealthy customers. Seeking a broader market, these houses created ready-to-wear fashions, still high-priced but positioned slightly lower than their haute couture lines. Fashion shifted from fine art to an industrial activity—ready-to-wear fashion was usually produced in small batches in job shops. Later, the fashion houses addressed the opportunities created by ready-to-wear for the growing upper-middle market. Haute couture designers rolled up their silk sleeves and created upper-middle price range "diffusion brands" that translated their high-end images to broader markets. Dolce & Gabbana's D&G; Calvin Klein's CK; Giorgio Armani's Emporio Armani and Armani Exchange; Versace's Versus; and Prada's Miu Miu were launched to capture different upper-middle market segments.

At the same time, as illustrated by figure 2-2, by the early 1990s, some mass marketers were moving *up* to the lower-middle price range market. Sweden's H&M and Italy's Benetton extended some of their lines to push a number of their products up. Retailers such as

FIGURE 2-2

The development of the European women's fashion industry

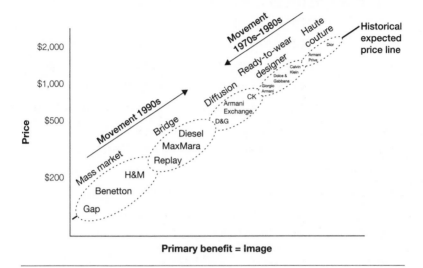

Primary benefit = Image

Replay and Diesel emerged in Europe using "bridge" brands, which were characterized by brand names with distinctive and fashionable images but not attached to a specific designer. The brand, not the designer, was the identity of the company. And their products were produced in large numbers.

And then came fast fashion. Zara, which opened its first store in La Coruña, Spain, in 1975, used superior production technologies and supply chain management to imitate ready to wear fashion. Zara's model threatened the mass, bridge, and diffusion brands by offering better quality and style but at lower prices. Zara was able to do this by creating a time-compressed production process that has become the subject of many business school case studies. Zara stores—and there are now over thirteen hundred in seventy-two countries—receive two deliveries a week. Each delivery includes new models, so what the stores offer is constantly changing. With over two hundred designers of its own, Zara identifies the trends of haute couture and ready-to-wear, then moves these fashions to the middle market in about four weeks, compared with the six months needed by old technology and processes.

Imitation within four weeks threw the bridge and diffusion brands off their stride. Previously, the fashion firms issued fall and spring collections; but when Zara had imitations available in mid-season, these firms were forced to issue new mid-season designs to differentiate themselves from Zara, leaving them with more excess inventory mid-season. Consequently, they were forced to dump this inventory on discount channels. In the past, buyers got last season's designs in the discount channels, but now they buy current-season designs at lower prices than the bridge and diffusion brand producers originally intended to charge. This further eroded their image at a time when they needed to distinguish themselves from Zara. Figure 2-3 shows the effect of Zara's pressure on the market.

Consumer responses to these trends also have brought different parts of the market into closer competition. In *Trading Up*, Michael

FIGURE 2-3

Zara puts pressure on other segments in the women's fashion industry in Europe by shifting the line

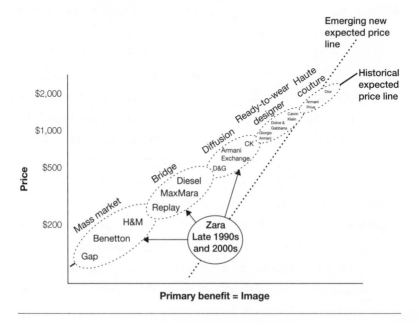

Primary benefit = Image

Silverstein and Neil Fiske note that consumers are accessorizing low-priced items such as Zara pants with a high-quality (diffusion-level) top or jewelry from a high-end designer.[3] The mass and luxury markets are more and more in competition with each other as fashion trends allow more freedom to mix and match, not just on colors and style, but also among prestige levels.

Zara has experienced tremendous growth and rising market power. By 2007, it was the biggest fashion company in Europe, outpacing H&M as the queen of cheap chic. With annual sales of €6,264 million (2007), it is committed to continuing international expansion. In 2008, Korea, Ukraine, Montenegro, Egypt, and Honduras were conquered, and, in 2009, Zara announced a joint venture with Tata Group to open stores in India starting in 2010.

MORE TO COME

Research by McKinsey shows that as long ago as 2002, bargain value retailers already accounted for more than 21 percent of the U.S. apparel market.[4] This trend would only increase in this and other markets. There are going to be companies like Zara emerging in a host of other industries. Global competition, the advent of new business models, new manufacturing processes, and the rise of off-shoring continue to create opportunities for low-end competitors to appear and take over markets. Half the population of consumers in the United States and Europe shops at value retailers such as Wal-mart (up from a quarter in 1996).[5] Many other industries are experiencing a "shift to value"—something that will be exacerbated by the recent global downturn, But this started long before the downturn, and will continue even in better times.

For example, Geico—the funky name for the Berkshire Hathaway–owned Government Employees Insurance Company—is busy swallowing up the insurance market, based on a low-price promise and clever marketing in which characters from cavemen to geckos offer reminders about how easy it is to use the company's online services and how to remember its unusual name. Geico has eroded and undermined the positions of traditional competitors, destroying their pricing power and differentiation, leading to commoditization in the auto insurance industry. Geico is now the fastest-growing major U.S. auto insurer, with 8.5 million policyholders.

Rubbermaid once was the dominant domestic player in the plastic goods market, offering surprisingly high-quality, durable products—from doghouses to garden sheds to kitchen storage containers to children's toys. It earned *Fortune*'s Most Admired Company award a few years running in the mid-1990s. But Rubbermaid sold through Walmart, which had realized that Chinese manufacturers could make unbranded plastic goods far more cheaply than Rubbermaid could. Rubbermaid's position deteriorated until it was bought by Newell. Similarly, when Corel and Corningware plates and dishes were hurt by cheaper Chinese rivals, Corning spun off its consumer products group, which ultimately went bankrupt.

The dilemma for managers is that they cannot compete head-to-head with these competitors and hope to win, yet if they stand still they will certainly lose share. Imitation of the imitator is not an option, and escape seems nearly impossible. Movement away from the low-end rival tends to back firms into smaller and smaller niches, while movement toward the rival (imitating and benchmarking it) leads to a no win game. Often a firm can't match its low-end rival's economies of scale, cost structure, and experience curve, so it loses the race. Even if it could match its rival's position, doing so would only serve to accelerate the deterioration when the low end discounter uses its muscle to punish all challengers.

STRATEGIES FOR RESPONDING TO DETERIORATION

How can companies respond to deterioration? What should you do if the entire market is moving toward the low end? The answer comes from the problem: as low end discounters gain market power, their rivals must reduce or manage the market power of the dominant discounter by sidestepping, undermining, or containing or controlling the discounters.

Escape the Trap: Sidestep the Discounter

In a battle with a dominant low-end discounter, sometimes discretion is the better part of valor. Some companies can shift their positions to *sidestep* the market power of the low-end discounter by making its power irrelevant or by avoiding its power. There are several ways to accommodate or move out of the way of a firm gaining massive market power by low-end discounting. These include moving upscale, moving away, and moving on.

Move Upscale

The first way to sidestep the market power of a firm that's driving market deterioration is to move upscale, conceding the low-end position to the discounter. For instance, some fashion firms have conceded the low and mid segments of the market and are moving upscale or away from the parts of the market where Zara has the most market power. In this way, the haute couture and ready-to-wear companies hope to perform a neat sidestep by moving into other high-end areas to keep their exclusivity. Some companies, such as Hermès, avoided the low-end threat by focusing entirely on high-end luxury goods that are classics rather than seasonal or annual fashion statements. Hermès reduced the number of its licensees and the stores carrying its goods to increase its exclusivity. Diesel and Chanel pursued a similar strategy.

Others are choosing unique materials to sidestep Zara, such as Diesel's focus on building expertise and dominance in denim products. Some high-end brands are also using rare fibers such as "baby cashmere," which comes from the first combing of a young goat, requiring about twenty goats to make a single sweater. This is a place where mass-producing low-end players cannot follow.

When the demand for luxury goods remains solid, thanks to the stability of the distribution of wealth among the rich, staying focused on this target segment can keep high-end brands out of Zara's reach. Brands using this strategy emphasize exclusivity to clearly separate themselves from the low end. In some rare instances, the move can be so successful that it actually reverses the deterioration by drawing the market upscale away from the discounter.

The silk industry in Italy—responsible for over 90 percent of European silk production—successfully competed against low-cost Chinese rivals by concentrating on high-value-added positions. As a result, during one period of eight months, exports of Italian silk to China *increased* by 155 percent, despite the availability of low-cost silk from China.

Part of the secret of success in Italian silk making has been several initiatives to move upscale and redefine benefits for customers. Small Italian silk makers in the northern Italian city of Como, for example, joined together to create a new brand that gave them the scale and marketing to compete more effectively in global markets. These companies also co-invested in new technologies to produce higher-quality fabrics that don't tear, irritate skin, or stain. They are changing how quality is defined for certain segments of the market, allowing them to effectively meet the Chinese challenge. The Italian manufacturers were also able to add convenience, innovation, and flexibility to their services. This allowed them, at least in the short term, to utilize the sidestep strategy—moving away from the pull of the market power of low-end players. Instead of trying to beat the low-end rivals—a competition that Italian silk makers were ill prepared for—they moved up out of the line of fire.

Move Away

Unless moving upscale is movement into a large or growth segment, moving upscale may not be enough. If so, companies can also move away from direct competition with the low-end player by changing channels, time, or place. For example, Procter & Gamble's Iams brand and Hill's Pet Nutrition's Science Diet were initially sold through vets and specialty pet stores to avoid competition with large competitors such as Purina in the supermarkets. While coffee brands such as Folgers were fighting bitter price wars in the super-markets for what had been seen as a commodity product, Howard Schultz created Starbucks as an entirely new channel for brewed coffees and beans, breaking free of commoditization until Starbucks over-saturated the market with too many stores.

End runs can also be achieved by moving to new geographies. When Southwest came into the domestic airline market, major carriers focused more attention on international routes where Southwest was not a problem. While the low-end players are using less-well-known brand names, the same pattern of accommodation can be seen in oral care products. While Colgate and P&G share the market in the United States, Colgate is the dominant player in many places overseas, enjoying more than a 70 percent share in many foreign countries. Under Reuben Mark's leadership, Colgate divested itself of many unrelated business units and refocused on its core—oral care products. The company staked a solid claim in the global toothpaste market and proved many times that it would react aggressively if competitors tried to infiltrate its international strongholds. It is interesting to note that, while Colgate doesn't promote its noncore brands aggressively overseas or in the United States, the firm continues to retain these brands as toehold positions just in case the competition decides to move into its strongholds. Colgate has accommodated P&G and other rivals in the American domestic market but chosen to fight its battles abroad. By moving away, Colgate has enjoyed a long record of strong, stable, steady growth in earnings per share and an incredibly impressive appreciation in its stock price until the 2008 credit crunch.

Move On

Many haute couture companies are sidestepping Zara's market power by moving out of fashion clothing to avoid the deterioration there, instead investing more of their attention on other very high-end products. They are designing everything from designer hotels and restaurants (Armani, Bulgari, Versace, and others); consumer electronics and appliances (Armani is working with Samsung); cell phones (Prada is in partnership with LG); automobiles (Versace is designing the interiors of Lamborghinis); helicopters (Armani and Versace are designing the interiors of helicopters created by AgustaWestland); furniture (Armani Casa); and even floral arrangements at branded florist shops (Armani Fiori). Armani, in particular, is attempting to create a unique lifestyle and customer experience called the "Armani Lifestyle." It is an appeal to the very wealthy, using products so high end and unique that they do not compete with Zara, nor can they be imitated by Zara's mass production and sourcing system.

Sometimes companies exit from the market of a low-end competitor completely. When Asian companies began taking over the memory chip industry, Intel realized it could not compete on price so it shifted to making microprocessor chips for personal computers. When it faced newly competitive followers in microprocessors such as AMD during the late 1990s and cheap Asian microprocessors in the early 2000s, Intel moved to making chips for consumer electronics and other special applications.

When he took the helm as CEO in the mid-2000s, Paul Otellini realized that Intel needed to look beyond personal computers to growth markets, such as consumer electronics and health care, to escape the commodity trap of low-end players. He created the first new slogan for the company in many years: "Leap ahead." The leap was spearheaded with Intel's Viiv chip for consumer electronics (with the potential to draw together the home PC, TiVo, stereo, and cable television). Alliances with Cisco in networking and Motorola in wireless communications were established. Chips for digital medical systems for hospitals and remote health monitoring at home were developed. Intel also introduced its dual core chips into Apple computers for the first time, and was developing chips for devices from BlackBerrys to iPods. To prime the company to launch more products than ever before in its history, Intel hired twenty thousand new employees, including a bevy of anthropologists to shake up the engineering firm (one output from the anthropologists is Intel's Technology Metabolism Index, which charts technology adoption). In the face of overwhelming deterioration in its core market, Intel appeared to be preparing to escape to new products or new markets. In February 2009, the company unveiled plans to invest $7 billion in U.S. factories that will make new, 32-nanometer chips and support seven thousand high-tech jobs.

Another approach to moving on is to redefine your target segment and create products with primary benefits that fit that segment, as appears to have happened in the increasingly commoditized chewing-gum business. When Wrigley's traditional brands were imitated and underpriced, or sold alongside a lot of discounted candy, Wrigley saw its market share shrink. So Wrigley moved on to a new set of hot sugar-free brands, such as Orbit, which was differentiated based on innovation and functional attributes such as breath freshening, teeth whitening, or serving as a low-calorie snack.[6]

By mid-2007, traditional gums were losing market share, with Doublemint declining 5 percent over the year before, JuicyFruit down 19 percent, and Bubblicious and Bubble Yum off 21 percent and 11 percent, respectively. On the other hand, the popularity of the new sugar-free gums grew. Sales of Orbit, the market leader, had rocketed ahead 23 percent, Trident Splash grew by 103 percent, and Cadbury Adams's Stride expanded by more than 1,000 percent.

To keep ahead of this new game and help to shape the new primary benefit, Wrigley launched a $45 million Global Innovation Center in Chicago in 2005. Among its next-generation creations, it developed a high-concept offering called "5" that promises to "stimulate your senses." So the move to sidestep the fierce competition in the traditional segment actually led to a new growth segment that is replacing the traditional segment.

Destroy the Trap: Undermine the Discounter

The second way to beat a commodity trap is to attack it. Probably the hardest but also the most rewarding way to destroy a deterioration trap is to *undermine* the market power of the low-end discounter.

One way to undermine a competitor is to erode its power from below by offering even lower prices and benefits through a reinvented value chain that still generates profits. Another strategy is to redefine the way customers see price. Say a company is taking share by selling a very inexpensive product, such as an almost "disposable" car with very low product durability and easily replaceable engines and other parts to extend its life. The perceived purchase price of these cars could be increased, and the market share of the firm decreased, if rivals convince customers to look at the total cost of ownership, including repair and replacement costs, over the long term. So the perceived price of the product is redefined to include more than the initial purchase price.

Redefine Value

Companies can undermine the discounter by staking out a new position that is even lower or by fighting to neutralize the advantage of the discounter. Even if a new low-end competitor is moving in, there are many ways to create positions that undermine the rise of the entrant by attacking its low-cost or quality position. This can be done through simplified design, the stripping out of product benefits, or a reinvented value chain that lowers costs. Alternatively, a company can challenge the value proposition of the low-end rival.

In the fashion industry, for example, some companies are using celebrities and advertising to raise their image and directly undermine the value proposition of discount players. European mass retailer H&M is trying to neutralize Zara's model of designerless fast fashion imitations by offering low-priced products while using stars such as Madonna and guest designers such as Karl Lagerfeld, Stella McCartney, and Roberto Cavalli to raise its image. The goal is to undermine Zara by offering more for a lower or similar price. In addition, H&M is redesigning its store formats to look more attractive than Zara's stores in Europe. H&M displays its clothing on shiny steel racks, which look more upscale than the boxes and bins through which many European Zara customers have to search.

Fashion-forward players such as Gucci and Dior use innovation and speed to undermine or match Zara's advantage in imitation, making half their sales from new products each year, compared with about 20 percent on average for less-fashion-forward firms. By rapidly introducing products and repositioning brands to have clearer positions and better-defined customer segments, customers are buying the intangible brand image, uniqueness, and emotional content of Gucci and Dior products, making Zara's emphasis on imitating the physical product less effective.

These firms are not running away from Zara. They are making themselves fast enough to partially neutralize Zara's advantage by making imitation more difficult. They now issue eight collections per year rather than two, as they once did. Gucci Groupe (owned by French conglomerate PPR) is repositioning its collection of brands (Gucci, YSL, Bottega Veneta, Alexander McQueen, Stella McCartney, and Balenciaga) to get more consistency and to clarify each brand's image and target market.

Armani and other major designers like Dolce & Gabbana now preview portions of their collections in private showings to manufacturers and retailers. As a result, they sell most of their designs in secret well before they hit the runway, preempting Zara's imitation of their designs after they become publicly released. Some 60 to 70 percent of Armani revenues are attributable to such "pre-collection" sales.

Another potential way to undermine Zara's value proposition is through selling used clothing. While high-fashion houses are fighting for new clothing, there has been a rapid expansion of the market for used clothing. In the United States, the small, unorganized stores in this sector are being replaced with more organized chains. For example, "pre-owned" designer clothing chain Buffalo Exchange, with thirty-four stores nationally, did $56 million in revenue in 2008. Is this the CarMax of the clothing industry? Is there an opportunity for the high-end brands to create their own "pre-owned" fashion business in Europe, as Toyota did with certified pre-owned Lexus cars?

For example, in many cases haute couture and ready-to-wear garments have been worn only once before being discarded by their wealthy buyers, so there is room to create used-clothing stores that are not vintage stores. A designer could offer trade-in credits for used clothing toward the purchase of another used item or even a new high-end dress. And since there is no wear and tear to speak of, customers can purchase a relatively recent dress at a low price. This would undermine discounters such as Zara.

Automation can obviously change the cost structure of an industry. But the surprise is that even service industries are being automated and industrialized with outsourcing, off shoring, software, and new operational processes.[7] Take the car-repair business. The vast majority of car repairs and bodywork was typically done in small, dirty, mom-and-pop shops that offered work of dubious quality, using pirated parts for a discounted price. Countering these low-end discounters were the high-priced car dealers that used genuine factory parts, all the latest diagnostic tools, and highly trained technicians; but many customers avoided them, fearing that these shops' real purpose was to convince consumers that they needed to buy a new car. Now, specialty chains have emerged that use automation to industrialize their service, undermining the low-end providers by charging less than the independents while offering a more professional image, faster turnaround, better service, and higher customer satisfaction.[8] Assembly-line procedures have been employed in both repair and bodywork by specialist firms. Thus, even when faced with a low-end competitor, companies sometimes have opportunities to undermine them by staking out an even lower position.

Redefine Price

Another way to undermine the market power of a low-end discounter is to redefine price. The key to a low-end discounter's market power is its price, which drives market share. As it continues to drive down prices, the discounter destroys rivals and increases it scale, further lowering its costs. One way to undermine this power is to change customer perceptions of pricing. For example, frequent flier miles in airlines helped to offset the low prices of no-frills competitors by bundling the price of the ticket with future free travel.

There are many opportunities to switch the way customers see prices during a purchase decision without redefining the primary benefit or having to strip off secondary benefits. By focusing on the total cost of ownership (including energy, financing, repairs, downtime, and other operating expenses) rather than just the initial purchase price, GE has fought off lower-priced rivals in numerous businesses during the 2000s, including the locomotive and large turbine markets. GE bundles financing, repair services, and other services into the purchase price, making the total life-cycle cost of its products lower than its rivals'.

Companies can also give away the product or sell it at a very low price, then make their money on recurring revenues. Adobe gives away Acrobat Reader for its popular PDF format, but charges for software to create Acrobat files. Companies also can give away the product and charge a usage fee as is done with products from copiers (based on copies made) to leased automobiles (based on miles driven). Companies also charge for results. Consulting firms and other service organizations are now charging not by the hour or the project, but for the performance improvements that they deliver to their clients.

Another way to change pricing is to charge a membership fee but keep product prices low; warehouse clubs such as BJ's and Costco do this. Sometimes companies use complexity in a way that makes it hard for customers to compare pricing, as with cell phone plans, medical insurance, or airline tickets. (Of course, this creates opportunities for another redefinition of prices based on simplified pricing.) These are just a few of the ways that pricing moves can be used to contain the market power of a low-end discounter.

Turn the Trap to your Advantage: Contain and Control the Discounter

The third way to beat a deterioration trap is to turn it to your advantage. In this strategy, companies work to *contain* the market power of the discounter to a limited part of the market.

Contain by Surrounding

The power of the low-end discounter can be contained by establishing positions around it—in effect creating a proliferation trap, as discussed in chapter 3. Consider what was happening to Walmart before the recession.

Target drew away some of Walmart's market share by emphasizing design and style over price alone. Meanwhile, Costco and BJ's Wholesale Club changed pricing to undermine Walmart's market power, using membership fees to consistently offer merchandise at lower prices than Walmart superstores. The clubs focused on a limited selection of high-volume items that allowed them to sell the most popular trip-generating products for less.

Krogers, the largest independent grocery chain in the United States, also had success in challenging Walmart's entry into the grocery business. Using slightly lower prices and improved customer service, Krogers continued to grow in the face of a threat from more than one hundred Walmart Superstores.[9] Kroger's has a "Customer

1st" strategy which, it says, focuses on four things: "Our people are great!; I get the products I want, plus a little; the shopping experience makes me want to return; and our prices are good."[10] Using this strategy, Krogers increased market share in thirty-seven of its forty-four major markets in 2007 and recorded sales of $70,235 million, up 6 percent.

In essence, Walmart's rivals used a proliferation trap to contain for several years the deterioration trap Walmart had created. But since deterioration in the market was rejuvenated by the recession that started in 2008, Walmart once again gained the upper hand. As people's incomes shrink, they no longer seek proliferation, returning instead to the basics offered by low-end discounters.

Nevertheless, a swarm of rivals, particularly small ones, can turn the inflexibility and weight of the large company against it. For example, when clothing discounters like T.J. Maxx and the wholesale clubs pushed into the low-end clothing markets, Walmart began to try to compete in fashion. But it was fighting with a disadvantage. Walmart had trouble stocking stores with the right sizes for its customers because its customers typically wear much larger sizes than those made by fashion houses sold at the wholesale clubs and T.J. Maxx.

As rivals buzz around its ears, avenues for the expansion of the low-end discounter can be blocked. As specialists surrounded it, Walmart's growth slowed during the mid 2000s. Due to its already large number of sku's, Walmart was unable to expand its assortment to match the specialists without increasing inventory costs and the costs of increased complexity in its purchasing and distribution functions.

Microsoft has staved off containment by specialists by bundling numerous applications, such as Microsoft Office, browsers, and security software into its operating systems. In security software, Microsoft's bundling strategy poses a tremendous threat to stand-alone software makers such as Symantec and McAfee. By offering security products such as firewalls and antivirus programs for free, Microsoft makes it impossible for rivals to compete on price.[11] This type of deterioration is tough to beat, as companies such as Lotus and Netscape discovered. But many companies have beaten "free" by containing it at the low end of the market; examples include bottled water versus tap water, and private health care providers versus free government health care providers (for example, the Veteran's Administration).

Intuit, for instance, beat back Microsoft by using speed to contain Microsoft Money in accounting products by offering more responsive customer service and the ability to keep up with fast-changing tax and accounting rules. Symantec and McAfee are responding by adding features that Microsoft doesn't offer. McAfee is adding software that provides improved security management for computer systems administrators who want to establish and enforce policies about the degree of protection and access to various machines, types of data, and software. While Microsoft is protecting the operating system, Symantec is protecting information, and in the future might offer more protection in other areas such as interactions and identity.

Of course, Microsoft could imitate these moves but not so easily as you might think. Both accounting/tax and security software requires expertise and frequent and timely updating that is difficult for a behemoth like Microsoft to provide. These constraints help to contain and block Microsoft's market power from some parts of the software market.

Companies can also use a geographic brand of containment. D&G is expanding the number of its company-owned boutiques around the world to compete better against companies such as Zara. By taking back control from licensees, D&G hopes to be able to execute its strategies against the discounter more quickly and forcefully. Benetton expanded its network of fifty-five hundred stores and increased its fashion cycles to four per year while reworking its image through advertising and new store design to try to contain the threat of Zara to the low end. At the same time, H&M is also beginning to contain Zara to its customer niche by introducing a series of specialized stores targeting different segments, such as children's clothing, accessories, and lingerie, to surround Zara.

Some diffusion brands, such as Roberto Cavalli's Just Cavalli and Gianfranco Ferre's GF Ferre, are reducing their prices to contain Zara as well. At the same time, Chloé offered lower prices through its new See brand.

Legal maneuvering is another strategy for containment. Chloé, for example, is defending its diffusion designs against imitators using lawsuits, such as the one filed against UK-based Topshop (the UK chain was forced to destroy over one thousand of its dresses that copied a £185 Chloé design) and another against Kookaï for selling copycat versions of its snakeskin Silverado handbags.

Control by Moving Customers in the Market

A low-end discounter can also be controlled by *moving customers* to an upscale value proposition. This is more than moving the firm upscale—not only does the firm move its products upmarket, but it also redefines the market by taking its customer base with it, leaving the discounter with a shrinking market niche. As mentioned earlier, sometimes the sidestep move—if supported with clever repositioning and innovation—can be so successful that companies find a way to draw the entire market upward, essentially reversing the deterioration caused by the low-end competitor. In essence, the company moves upscale to escape the trap and in doing so migrates customers to the upper end of the market. This is a difficult strategy to implement, but when possible it avoids the danger of allowing the low-end discounter to grab more market share and power, forcing powerless non-discounters to become trapped in the gilded cage of a high-end niche. Instead of merely moving upscale and leaving much of the market behind with the low-end discounter, firms using this strategy take the market with them by offering a high-end product at a price below the expected price line.

This approach was successfully used by Gillette in meeting the challenge of the low-end entry of BIC disposable razors. The disposables took away share from Gillette's higher-priced cartridge razors, which offered more benefit (closer shave) at a higher price. Gillette first responded by matching the move at the low end with its own disposable Good News razor, launched in 1976. But margins were so tight that, even though Gillette was successful in gaining share, this move contributed to the deterioration trap that BIC had created. Gillette's profits deteriorated, and its success in disposables became a pyrrhic victory: Gillette narrowly avoided a hostile takeover in the 1980s.

Instead of continuing to fight it out in the brutally price-sensitive low-end, Gillette turned to raising the bar at the high end, starting with the Sensor. It offered such a compelling price-benefit position that Gillette actually took market share away from the disposables, deteriorating BIC's position from above. From this new starting point, Gillette then went on to drive the process of escalation (as described in chapter 4), managing the momentum with a series of launches, including the Sensor, Mach3, and the Fusion models. Gillette always had its next-generation product waiting in the wings, and had at least one extension product to anticipate the moves of followers—for example, the Sensor Excel, the Mach3 Turbo, and M3Power. Its innovations have raised the bar on safety, smoothness, and closeness of shaving. Yet with Fusion, it appears that Gillette may be running out of room to keep driving the momentum, because how much closeness is too close? So Gillette had to look for a new way to change the game. By selling the company to P&G, Gillette can now tap into many new distribution strategies to gain market share, making new product development a less important feature of its strategy. But overall, what started out looking like an effort to make moot the low-end discounter's market power by moving upscale, ultimately contained and even reduced BIC's market power over the long run.

In some cases, deterioration becomes too hard to handle and there is no way to escape, destroy, or take advantage of it. This is especially true when deterioration is caused by a protracted economic downturn or other factors that evaporate a significant amount of demand. Under such circumstances, other strategies must be employed to survive (see "Deterioration and Demand Evaporation").

Deterioration and Demand Evaporation

A sharp economic downturn sometimes causes the perfect storm. Market prices and benefits deteriorate as customers feeling the pinch seek bargains—and demand simply evaporates. While technically not commoditization, this type of deterioration makes it particularly difficult for firms to improve their competitive position or pricing power by escaping, undermining, or using the deterioration. In such situations, additional measures must be taken to survive the hurricane, including:

- *Batten down the hatches to weather the storm by protecting the firm's core business.* This includes measures such as getting back to basics by pruning low-profit products and geographies or segments, decreasing discretionary spending, cutting excess capacity to prop up prices, reducing costs (through layoffs, more efficient processes, restructuring, and other such measures), and doing only the essentials necessary to survive. The goal is to maximize cash flow from core operations. Aggressive management of the top line is required as well. Customers must be convinced that the firm's products are a basic necessity to compete with rivals, or will solve or prevent a major problem that the company might face in the future. The sales force may be directed to bypass purchasing agents to

discuss sales with higher-level executives. Products or
processes may be imported from emerging markets into the
core business to capture emerging market knowledge about
low-cost processes and low-end products. Firms will typically keep prices low, but not start or exacerbate price wars.

- *Prepare to float with the hurricane winds to absorb or avoid
  too much financial and strategic damage.* This is done by
  being proactive and moving before the problem worsens.
  To make it easier to absorb financial losses, firms lower
  their breakeven points by reducing debt-to-equity ratios,
  refinancing debt, reducing dividends and stock buybacks,
  and cutting fixed costs and assets, replacing them with
  variable costs or outsourcing. Firms unlock cash from their
  operations by cutting inventory and capital expenditures,
  stretching payables, and collecting receivables sooner. They
  often increase their strategic and operational flexibility
  and adjust their portfolios more quickly. Firms also reevalu-
  ate their risks from operations and their credit policies.
  The goal is to bite the bullet early in one large chunk rather
  than to suffer incremental loses as the firm makes reac-
  tionary incremental moves to adjust to increasing losses
  and declining demand.

- *Landing on your feet when the storm is over.* The best
  firms don't just react to the storm. They position for the future by selectively increasing their R&D during the storm to
  be ahead of competitors when the storm breaks. Some
  firms look for transformative mergers as rivals weaken during the shakeout, creating opportunities to consolidate or
  reduce capacity in key markets. Others improve customer
  service, or even invest in customers, relying on the idea
  that customers will remember the favor when the inevitable

recovery comes. Still others use the crisis to reinvent their business models and position for pent-up demand and the growth markets that will emerge after the downturn. They work with the government to create new regulations designed to prevent future downturns, but simultaneously raise barriers to entry for post-downturn potential entrants. And they anticipate the inflation that might occur when the government prints money to pay off recession-era government debts incurred by stimulus and bailout packages, or the impact on the working, middle and upper classes when taxes are increased and other benefits cut to help balance the budget.

I think it was put best by Winston Churchill, who once said: "If you are going through hell, just keep on going!"

FIGHT OR FLIGHT? YOU CHOOSE

The key decision about market power management strategies is whether to fight or flee. Like any schoolyard fight-or-flight decision, the choice is based on the relative strengths of your rivals (whether you think you can win the fight) and the opportunities for flight (if there is an escape route). Winning the fight depends on the resources you have to throw at the battle relative to the low-end competitor. If you are hopelessly outmatched, then the choice may be to flee if a sidestepping move is feasible. If you are evenly matched or have an advantage, then containing or undermining the discounter becomes more possible. It is not just your own resources that count, but also the resources of partners that you can pull into the fray. As Zara has gained market power in fashion, using its profits to expand rapidly, it has been harder for rivals to stop Zara, or even to keep up. Fear of retaliation may also affect whether rivals choose to confront or contain the low-end player. In brief, companies caught in the deterioration trap need to assess the balance of power between themselves and the low-end discounter.

If you can't win the fight with the low-end player, then the question is whether there is a route out. Can you aid someone else's effort to undermine the low-end discounter or find an ally to help, as IBM did to Dell by selling its PC division to low-cost Chinese manufacturer Lenovo? If you already have a high-end brand or product position, you must judge whether your position will be a safe haven or will be affected by the ripples made by the low-end discounter, as we saw in the fashion industry. If there are ripple effects, your position is tenuous, but it can still be used as a launch platform for moving away or moving on to avoid the deterioration caused by the discounter. The question is whether you can move on or away quickly enough before your market share in your old position is so depleted so that you lack the resources to make the move. If your brand is focused on a smaller niche or a safe haven, then the issue is whether you can find a way to expand the market for this brand. If there is no path out, then you might be forced to come up with a way to fight—even though you will be in an unfair fight with a behemoth. In many cases, industry consolidation, or an extensive network of alliance partners, may be needed to gain the critical mass required to fight the low-end discounter.

Finally, you must consider the costs and risks of flight. If you have a valuable brand, sidestepping may stop deterioration temporarily, but at the sacrifice of your long-term brand equity. Flight may also signal weakness to the competitor and lead it to pursue you more aggressively up the price-benefit line or in other markets, as Toyota did to GM by starting with small cars and moving up to SUVs, luxury cars, and recently into larger light trucks. So flight may just lead to another tougher fight in the future. All these factors will affect the choice of a strategy to battle deterioration.

While Zara offers much lower quality and prestige than its haute couture rivals, the market power of a dominant low-end player more than makes up for its downsides. This change can be seen in the rising fortunes of Zara's owner Amancio Ortega. With a net worth of $24 billion, he was Spain's richest man and number 8 on the 2007 *Forbes* global list of billionaires. The son of a railway worker, he got his start making gowns and lingerie in his living room more than four decades before founding Zara in 1975. His fortune places him ahead of Stefan Persson (17), the head of the H&M chain started by his father, and far in front of Giorgio Armani (177) and the Benettons (323). There is a lot of money to be found at the low end of the market.

Fighting the market power of a large and growing low-end discounter that is causing the entire market to deteriorate can make you feel like David fighting Goliath. Yet Napoleon Bonaparte's words remind us that "the essence of strategy is, with a weaker force, always to have more force at the crucial point than the enemy." And if we recognize a rising power, we can undermine or contain it before it can gather too much market power. One wonders why Sears did not imitate or buy discounter Home Depot before it ruined Sears's home improvement business. Or why one of the large retailers did not imitate or buy discounter Walmart before it gathered steam. As Leonardo da Vinci observed: "It is easier to resist at the beginning than at the end."

THREE

The Proliferation Trap

How to Manage Multiple Threats to Your Competitive Position

Proliferation, the second commodity trap, appears when new price-benefit positions proliferate, surround, and erode a product's value proposition by targeting smaller segments of the customer base. With the fragmentation of markets and new, more focused business models, competitors can target narrower segments or use substitutes that serve some of the same customer needs. Where there once were a few broad positions, there are now many narrower ones. Rivals use these new positions to slice away slivers of the market of broadly positioned incumbents.

It is ironic that extreme differentiation results in commoditization. But as firms produce many products that begin to overlap with each other, they threaten the uniqueness of each others' products. Consequently they must reduce price to hold on to market share, or lose market share to hold on to their price. This is the proliferation trap.

The dilemma for managers caught in the proliferation trap is that they cannot fight everyone, everywhere, all the time. They end up exhausted, pulled in all directions, and spread too thin. But if they don't react, and simply stick to their current core competencies and product markets—what they do best—they will be eaten alive by more focused competitors. Rivals put pressure on the pricing of a firm that is surrounded because these focused competitors compete more viciously in their narrower target zones (see figure 3-1).

Telltale signs of a proliferation trap are:

- Your market is increasingly fragmented; new offerings and variations are being introduced all the time.

- Your value proposition is being undermined by new offerings targeted at ever-narrower market niches.

- You are frustrated because you are being attacked on many fronts but lack the resources to fight marketing and

FIGURE 3-1

Chapter 3 summary: The proliferation trap

	Proliferation ↓↑ Price ↓↑ Benefits
Description The causes	Caused by multiple threats due to substitutes, imitators, market fragmentation and new product innovation. Open many new price-benefit positions, surrounding and eroding the firm's product uniqueness.
Dilemmas The challenges	You can't fight everyone everywhere, all the time. But if you don't, you are stung to death by a swarm of bees.
Symptoms How to identify	• Market fragmenting with new offerings • Rivals targeting narrowing niches • Unable to fight on all fronts • Pressure to cut prices just to keep existing customers
Solutions The strategies	**Managing Threats** To reduce the magnitude and number of threats faced, to conserve resources, or to build capability to fight a multifronted war
Escape the trap	*Select* your threats (narrow the fronts).
Destroy the trap	*Overwhelm* the threats.
Turn the trap to your advantage	*Outflank* (outproliferate) the threats.

innovation wars to defend your main product against all these incursions.

- Surrounded on all sides, you are under constant pressure to reduce your prices just to retain your existing customers.

SEARSUCKERS

To see how proliferation plays out, consider what happened with the retailer Sears. Sears faced the proliferation trap with the arrival of specialty catalogs, mall boutique stores, category killers, wholesale clubs, and the consolidation of high-end department stores. Sears' broad positioning was being nibbled away. By the mid-1990s, Sears was surrounded and being attacked on many fronts by firms offering different slivers of Sears' product offerings, but in greater depth.

At the high end of the line, Sears was challenged by the consolidation of regional department stores, such as Federated Department Stores, to create multichain national organizations with economies of scale in purchasing, more prestigious brand names, and higher-priced, better-quality merchandise offered in more elegant retail spaces. Sears also was attacked at the bottom end as Walmart and Kmart emerged to become a threat in the discount segment. Walmart, especially, used store locations, supply chain innovations, and aggressive negotiations with suppliers to drive down prices to remarkable levels.

Meanwhile, wholesale clubs such as Sam's Club, BJ's, and Costco offered yet another value position based on low-prices, bulk purchases, and a "treasure hunt" mentality, coupled with stripped-down service, displays, and many of the other trappings of retail stores. Other innovative companies created category killers, focusing on each of Sears's departments. Toys "R" Us hit the toy department. Chains such as Best Buy attacked Sears's strongholds in electronics and appliances. Retailers such as Ace Hardware, True Value, Home Depot, and Lowe's attacked Sears's historical strengths in hardware and home improvement with a greater variety of products and price-benefit points. Meanwhile, specialty catalogs such as Lands' End carved up Sears's mail-order catalog—the famous "Wish Book"— to be joined later by Internet retailers.

My research has found that the primary solution to the proliferation trap is *threat management*. Companies can avoid threats by choosing their battles, outflanking the proliferators by finding power vacuums and open spaces. Or they can select and overwhelm the threats by eliminating them, scaring them off, swallowing them up, crushing them, or outproliferating the proliferators.

Sears, in fact, did use some of these strategies, although they were inadequately funded or executed. Most importantly, however, Sears refocused itself. It conceded the basic low-end value position to Walmart, Kmart, and other discounters, exiting numerous product lines. It also abandoned its catalog but continued doing fulfillment for specialty catalog companies. It then repositioned its mall stores with the "Softer Side of Sears" campaign to compete against the premium department stores, and brought in upscale brands and new product categories to compete with the department stores. It created or relied on its own stand-alone stores designed to be category-killer offerings such as Sears Hardware, NTB (auto parts), furniture chains, and lawn and garden chains.

Even so, Sears was not sufficiently focused—it retreated to fight on too many fronts and stayed wedded to its old general-store formats for too long—and the proliferators won. Sears gave up on or sold off its stand-alone chains, which it had lacked the skill to manage, and focused back on the mall stores. But it had no second act after the initially successful Softer Side of Sears campaign. The company was ultimately acquired by Kmart, which was itself seeking to define a value position that could stave off the financial collapse it faced in its own battle with Walmart.

Sears defined the department-store category and sustained its business for approximately a century. But as many new price-benefit positions were staked out, Sears' position was eroded, along with much of the company's stock value. As I write, it is still facing financial difficulties.

PROLIFERATING HOTELS

The problem of the proliferation trap grows exponentially when market fragmentation explodes to the point where several or all segments of the market are overcrowded with similar, but not quite identical, competitors.

This proliferation can be seen in the hotel industry. In just over a year, at least twenty-four new hotel brands appeared, among them: Cambria Suites, Hotel Indigo, Hyatt Place, element, and NYLO (New York Lofts) were all launched. Proliferation offered a way out of organizing the market around the usual five-star ratings, but it also created new competitive threats for established brands as companies staked out new positions. In this case, incumbent companies fended off the attackers through their own proliferation. Established players created their own new offerings—think of Starwood Hotels & Resorts Worldwide's W and aloft brands. But there are many anti-proliferation strategies that work or fail under different conditions.

Another way to manage these threats is to target the positions with the least competitive intensity, essentially sidestepping or avoiding the threatening proliferators—engaging in a game of hopscotch to narrow the battle to selected and constantly shifting fronts. Threat management can involve avoiding rivals, confronting rivals on the fronts where the resistance is slightest, or preparing to fight on many fronts simultaneously. In the rest of this chapter I examine the proliferation trap and additional threat management strategies for meeting it.

Three-Star Heaven

To understand this process of proliferation, let's go back to the halcyon days of the early 1970s when the hotel chain Holiday Inn was at its glorious three-star peak. In June 1972, founder Kemmons Wilson's face smiled from the cover of *Time* magazine, because of the success of the chain he had created.[1] Holiday Inn had fourteen hundred hotels dotting American interstates. Each Holiday Inn was carefully located to be within a day's drive of the next. It was truly "the nation's innkeeper." It had even inspired Neil Diamond and Elton John to pen songs ("Holiday Inn Blues" and "Holiday Inn," respectively).

Holiday Inn was the quintessence of the mid-range offering. Wilson's commercial genius was to provide inexpensive, standardized family accommodations as an alternative to the sleazy independently owned motor courts of the era. Holiday Inn offered reliable clean sheets, air-conditioning, swimming pools, and friendly service. The chain dominated its part of the industry and set the standard for a host of rivals such as Ramada Inn, Howard Johnson's motor lodges, and Days Inn. Holiday Inn's "great sign" became a fixture of the American highway and a beacon for the family station wagons full of weary travelers.[2] It was a reliable three-star chain that was within family budgets but clearly separate from both the high-end luxury players or the fleabag dives at the bottom.

But when you're on top of the world, complacency—and commoditization—often creeps insidiously in. In 1975, Holiday Inn's slogan was: "The Best Surprise Is No Surprise," a reference to the chain's reliable service and quality. If only the industry had remained so simple: Holiday Inn was in for a few surprises of its own that would shake up its universe.

First, chains of two-star lodgings like Motel 6 and Quality Inn moved in from the bottom. These chains provided a standardized experience while competing on price with the three-star hotels and motels like Holiday Inn. At the same time, four-star chains emerged, offering some features that overlapped with those provided by the three-star establishments. Holiday Inn tried to respond by pushing itself up from three to four stars, dropping poorer-quality facilities and upgrading services. Slowed by its sunk investment in existing properties and its image, it was eaten alive by more nimble competitors. The company was bought by UK conglomerate Bass plc in 1988 (which later spun off its hotel operations as the InterContinental Hotels Group—IHG). It was the end of an era. Some of the old-style former Holiday Inns joined the two-star universe when their franchise agreements expired, finding a second life among chains such as Best Western or Days Inn.

Realigning the Stars

Positions in the hotel industry were once as clear as the set of stars that defined the relative quality of the chain (see "Hotel Star Ratings" for an overview of the ratings we used for our research). But the majority of the entrants in the late 1990s and early 2000s, which include Hyatt's Hyatt Place, and Starwood's aloft and element brands, are aimed at the upper end of the midscale to the lower end of the upscale market. The proliferation of new models for hotels and brands is characterized by lifestyle brands, positioned above their expected price lines. These lifestyle brands used brand image and different combinations of amenities to differentiate themselves from hotels at similar star ratings. Other chains repositioned to extend the expected price line at the extreme high end of the star range by adding six- and seven-star hotel chains with unique amenities and upscale services, including hotels designed by and named after Bulgari and Armani. The new Armani chain and Marriott's Bulgari Hotels are bringing in high-profile designers to push the upper limit of the hotel spectrum, with average daily room rates at a stratospheric $700 per night or above in exchange for a very elite experience.

Holiday Inn found its secure position at the mid range of the hotel universe undermined by this proliferation of new positions on the price-benefit map. For Holiday Inn, this proliferation resulted in an attack from the high end and the low end, eroding its average daily room rates, profit margins, and the uniqueness of its benefits. The result was commoditization in its segment.

Hotel Star Ratings

Price benefit segmentation in hotels is based on a set of standard star ratings[3]:

- *Super Luxury (7 stars):* Hotels with distinctive amenities or brands that place them above ordinary luxury hotels, as shown by much higher average daily rates, including Marriott's Ritz Carlton, Hilton's Waldorf Astoria, and Starwood's St. Regis and Luxury Collection.

- *Luxury (6 stars):* Hotels with a very high level of amenities, often boutiques or small chains with top-class facilities and services and very high room rates. A mix of business and leisure, depending on location, often with a high proportion of international guests.

- *Upper Upscale (5 stars):* Well-appointed hotels with full, high-quality amenities including spacious rooms and bathrooms, charging high room rates. Usually located in prime city-center locations in major cities or in resorts. Predominantly business, often with a high proportion of international guests.

- *Upscale (4 stars):* High-quality, mostly full-service hotels with moderate to high room rates. Less luxurious than upper upscale and sometimes lacking some of the facilities such as a concierge. Predominantly business in urban locations, but also appealing to the leisure guest; less international than upper upscale but can still have a significant international guest base.

- *Midscale (full service) (3 stars):* Full service but with fewer amenities than upscale. Comparatively lower room rates than upscale. Predominantly domestic guests, both business and leisure.

- *Midscale (limited service) (2 stars):* Reduced food and beverage, bar, and meeting facilities but room quality similar to full service midscale. Broadly comparable room rates with midscale (full service). Predominantly domestic guests, both business and leisure.

- *Economy/budget (1 star):* Cheapest, most basic hotels with limited facilities. Predominantly domestic guests.

These stars levels typically define the expected price line (based on average daily rates) for each hotel chain. However, some hotel brands appear above and below the chain's expected price line—typically the lifestyle hotels appear above the line and extended-stay suites below it. These companies are using other benefits to differentiate themselves from the traditional hotel brands on the company's star system-based expected price line.

How could hotel companies respond to these proliferation threats? Many took actions to confront the threats, most often by constructing a full-line portfolio of hotels that allowed them to compete in all the market segments. Bass's acquisition of Holiday Inn and other chains and new launches allowed it to meet the new competitive threats along the entire line, as illustrated in figure 3-2. In 1991, Bass, the holding company for the Holiday Inn and Inter-Continental Hotel chains as well as many other investments at the time, launched Holiday Inn Express as a brand to compete down-market, while only slightly discounting Holiday Inn's prices. The Crowne Plaza was introduced in 1994 to compete upmarket, fitting between the company's existing brands: Holiday Inn in the middle and InterContinental at the five-star end of the spectrum.[4] But the company remained centered firmly in the middle (three-star) position, even as Bass spun off IHG.

FIGURE 3-2

InterContinental Hotels Group

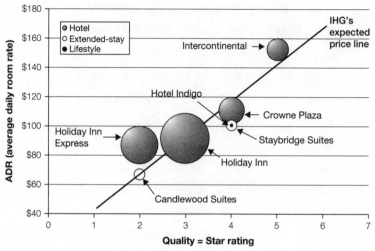

Circle size is proportional to number of rooms.

IHG's direct confrontation of multiple threats to protect its core market has been a costly and brutally competitive approach. Other companies carefully picked their positions along the full price line to select their battles, creating their portfolios to compete directly only in certain segments. Hilton Hotels Corporation, for example, was perhaps more successful in creating and managing this full-line response to the threats of proliferation, with average daily room rates that generally exceed IHG's at each star level. Hilton also did a better job of managing competition above and below its expected price line, especially at the important four-star level where it found successful niches at three price points. It also managed to attack IHG's core three-star market using the Hilton brand name but nevertheless minimized its exposure to the highly competitive and declining dead zone of three-star hotels by taking only a small position there. Basically, Hilton attacked IHG's three-star core but focused its

FIGURE 3-3

Hilton Hotels Group

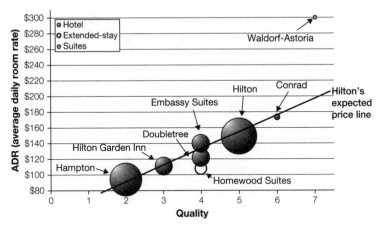

*ADR data estimated for Waldorf-Astoria.

resources on the higher and lower end of the star ratings (see figure 3-3).

Given the cost of fighting battles on many fronts, some companies selected the threats they would address even more carefully. Choice Hotels, for example, staked out positions at the one- and two-star end of the market, concentrating on competing for the budget traveler with many different franchised brands, including EconoLodge, Comfort Inn, Comfort Suites, and Quality Inn brands. It thus avoided having to sustain competition along many fronts and could concentrate its branding and marketing in one segment of the market. These moves put Choice Hotels in the best position for the late 2008 economic downturn.

At the other extreme, Starwood has focused on the high end (five-star hotels and above), including its Sheraton, Westin, and Le Méridien Chains, and its elite niche brands, such as the St. Regis and its one-of-a-kind Luxury Collection hotels. Starwood focused on the upscale traveler and the skills and marketing needed to attract this segment.

The strategic approach of Sears, in which the company chose its battles by selecting where to concede positions (e.g., catalogs) and where to fight (e.g., stand-alone category killers and mall stores), was similar to the way Hilton selected its battles. But Sears kept its focus on the general store (its middle-of-the-line format) and did not have the skill or resources to run the range of new formats and brands it selected. Unlike Hilton, Sears held on to a besieged format too long when it should have cut back more, using a more focused strategy (similar to Choice's or Starwood's).

Other hotel companies took actions to outflank the threats by moving off their expected price lines. Some chains created new brands based on new models. In the mid-1990s, for instance, companies created extended-stay offerings (usually called suites), catering to business travelers. These suites accepted slightly lower room rates in exchange for longer average stays, as shown in figures 3-2 and 3-3. Minor changes in secondary benefits made it possible to position above or below hotels with similar ratings.

Marriott's SpringHill Suites was designed to be an "upscale-ish" chain catering to business travelers seeking three-star accommodations. It does not offer full-service hotel amenities like the banquet rooms, extensive room service, concierge services, or fancy restaurants found at four-star hotels. On the other hand, it does offer indoor swimming pools, nice exercise rooms, and ergonomic workspaces not found at most three-star hotels.[5] And it charges a slight premium over the three-star hotels and a discount compared with the four-star hotels. Similarly, based on the ADRs (average daily rates), Marriott's Residence Inn is positioned at a discount compared with its other five-star hotels, the Marriott and Renaissance chains.

Lifestyle Choices

Another strategy used to outflank the threats at each star level was the move into lifestyle segmentation. This has been used most aggressively by Starwood. For example, brands such as W and aloft were able to charge rates above Starwood's expected price line for three-star and five-star levels, respectively, based on the experience they offered. Lifestyle segmentation targeted customers who wished to make a statement with their choice of accommodation. The new hotels featured living rooms and galleries, upscale restaurants and night clubs, avant-garde designs, and branded luxury fitting different life styles and tastes. Just as Starbucks transformed coffee from a product to an experience, the goal was to transform the hotel from a room to a unique experience targeted to specialty niches. These lifestyle hotels moved the industry from a product-centric view to a customer-centric view.

As Steve Heyer, then CEO of Starwood, explained to me:

The big "aha" for us was that demographic segmentation schemes didn't work. Guests with the same age, income, net worth, and number of family members were seeking different experiences. Demographics could not tell us about what the customer saw as a quality experience. We began segmenting based on emotions— how the customer wanted to feel in our different brands. The industry had been innovating relying on architecture and amenities, but this innovation was contextless. Segmentation and innovation based on unique promises that make people feel different, better, and special are key to a successful business.[6]

This was a different way of looking at the market. Instead of rating hotels using stars (based on facilities), the goal here was to create a *secondary benefit*: a better experience for different types of travelers. This process changed the way the industry looked at itself.

But even though Starwood was the early leader in lifestyle hotels, the company's management upheavals (including the departure of Heyer as CEO in April 2007) slowed its momentum. And there was another problem with trying to outflank the proliferation trap by staking out new positions. Once a new position is discovered, it typically doesn't remain free of rivals for very long. New threats ultimately appear. So it didn't take rivals long to catch on to Starwood's new game. As IHG CEO Andy Cosslett commented, "Hotels in the past have been segmented by price and not much else . . . Hotel brands in the future will have to stand for something."[7] All the major chains created their own extended-stay offerings and their lifestyle brands. They met proliferation with proliferation and this meant that the pathbreaker could outflank the others for only so long before commoditization came to call once again.

Signs of Change

In October 2007, InterContinental Hotels announced that it was investing $1 billion over three years, along with owners (most hotels are franchised), in a complete relaunch of the Holiday Inn chain of more than three thousand hotels. The initiative was intended to shift its focus from budget travelers to business travelers who already make up the bulk of its business so as to compete more effectively with chains such as Courtyard by Marriott, Hampton Hotels, and Hilton Garden Inn.[8] Holiday Inn is replacing bedding, adding curved shower curtain rails, and shuttering more than one hundred underperforming hotels per year. The changes go right down to a "scent and music" strategy with a subtle but distinctive Holiday Inn smell—a trend started by Starwood with its Sheraton and Westin brands.[9] InterContinental expects the renovated hotels to generate significantly higher revenue per available room. The new hotels also are moving to a new logo, which replaces the script "Holiday Inn" with a simple white "H" on a green square.[10] (While the chain's name remains the same, the new logo evokes the simple elegance of Starwood's W brand, one of the pathbreakers in the proliferation movement.)

The hotel industry has become a fierce battleground; new brands and business models have proliferated, each with different approaches to segmentation of the market. In proliferation environments, the one strategy that clearly will not work is standing still—as Holiday Inn found out. Standing still means being left behind, surrounded by proliferation and finding room rates falling and commoditization creeping in from all sides. As Steve Porter, the head of Holiday Inn's U.S. operations, said with the announcement of the relaunch plan, "Our relevance is at risk."[11] The three-star segment seems to be a dying segment of the market. With Holiday Inn as the dominant player in the segment, IHG's center of gravity is in the wrong place. Can the company correct it? Will the makeover of Holiday Inn be enough in the face of economic downturn and the complex competitive battlefield created by the proliferation? Some might say that it is caught irretrievably in the proliferation trap, and its makeover is a day late and a dime short.

STRATEGIES FOR RESPONDING TO PROLIFERATION

As the hotel industry powerfully demonstrates, proliferation can undermine positions and lead to commoditization as new competitive positions threaten existing ones, eroding margins. My research has found that the way to counter this proliferation is to *manage the threats.*

As illustrated by the hotel example, there are three primary ways that companies manage threats. They escape the proliferation trap by *selecting threats*, as Choice and Starwood did in focusing on low-end and high-end hotels, respectively. Second, they can attack and *overwhelm the threats*, choosing to fight on many fronts, as Hilton did by creating brand extensions and a full-line portfolio. Finally, they can turn the trap to their advantage by *outflanking* their rivals by engaging in their own proliferation to open new positions (as with the lifestyle, high-end niche, and extended-stay brands) above or below the line, or at the extremes of the expected price line.

Escape the Trap: Select Your Threats

Sometimes proliferation threats cannot be confronted directly. In these cases, companies can still narrow the battle by selection of certain threats to focus on, as we saw with the focus of Choice Hotels on the one- and two-star end of the market.

Companies often select the areas where there is the least resistance from rivals—either positions on the price-benefit map with low competitive intensity or positions where the company has some tremendous advantage over rivals. Companies can also move in and out of less competitively intense areas as they appear and disappear, as is often done in the auto and the consumer packaged goods industries.

Sometimes companies can fight proliferation by jumping quickly into segments that will be profitable or growth positions—as they come and go—before rivals have a chance to recognize these opportunities. (In contrast to white space, discussed later, these positions are not new positions on the map but rather existing positions where competition is less fierce.)

Destroy the Trap: Overwhelm the Threats

When the threat of the proliferators cannot be escaped by selection or outflanking, then firms have to be prepared to fight. Two issues must be considered in planning these fights. First is whether to divide or concentrate resources—that is, whether to use multiple strategies against multiple fronts (as Hilton did with its strong full-line portfolio) or to find one universal strategy that addresses all of them. The second issue is timing, whether to confront the threats simultaneously or sequentially.

Concentrate Your Resources

Instead of fighting different proliferators on many fronts—a very resource-intensive approach—companies with fewer resources can sometimes find a single position that defends against a variety of threats at the same time. Carefully analyzing a firm's benefits relative to different competitors can help to create a defensible position against each rival individually and simultaneously. BJ's Wholesale Club, the number-three wholesale club in the United States, concentrated primarily on the East Coast, created such a strategy to meet the proliferation of a variety of rivals. It had the unenviable position of facing many successful and aggressive rivals such as Costco, and Walmart's Sam's Club and Supercenters, as well as numerous supermarket chains and category killers. BJ's successfully created a defensible set of benefits by focusing its resources on the East Coast and selecting its targets prudently (especially the much-higher-priced, inefficient grocery chains). It also differentiated itself from the supercenters, category killers (such as Best Buy), supermarkets, and other warehouse clubs with just one primary format that could be scaled down in size as needed for more rural local markets.

Like other warehouse clubs, BJ's differentiated itself from grocery chains and Walmart Supercenters by stripping away many of the traditional trappings of retailing, lowering prices and using membership fees to keep product prices low. BJ's then added points of differentiation by focusing on fresh foods, lobster tanks, wider variety, high-quality brands, and exclusive-looking private labels, as well as offering smaller package sizes and more payment options. This positioning resulted in BJ's having not just one position, but multiple simultaneous ones, each designed to defend against the different proliferators surrounding its position, as illustrated in figure 3-4.

BJ's reduced its conflict with Costco, which focused more on small businesses, by concentrating on upscale family segments, particularly women. BJ's has successfully taken on Walmart's Supercenters, charging on average 15 percent below the Supercenters' prices by using the best logistics and labor costs in the wholesale club market, with lower-cost operations than even Costco. It has used segmentation to avoid Sam's Club customers, who tend to be

FIGURE 3-4

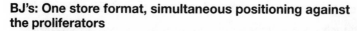

BJ's: One store format, simultaneous positioning against the proliferators

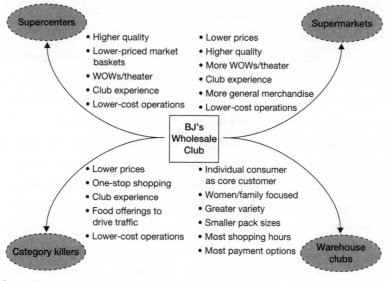

Source: Used with permission of BJ's Wholesale Club CEO Mike Wedge.

penny pinchers with an average income of $35,000, by focusing on segments with income averaging over $80,000.

But BJ's biggest target was supermarkets, where it achieved prices that were 30 percent lower on an overall market basket. BJ's has expanded its fresh foods offerings, introducing lobster tanks in many stores, taking shelf space from general merchandise to expand offerings that compete with supermarkets, adding gas stations and pharmacies, and even testing out child-friendly environments with three-story play centers and babysitting. This has made it very difficult for supermarkets to follow, given their lack of space and smaller formats. BJ's often exceeds the same-store sales growth and profitability of both Costco and Sam's Club. Overall, BJ's resorted to a "one-size-fits-all" approach to take on the proliferators because it lacked the size and resources to split into specialists that can take the offensive against some and defend against others.

Create a Wolf Pack

In contrast to BJ's unified approach, a company with a generalist or broad position and significantly large and diverse resources can break itself into smaller pieces that can act more nimbly in fighting the proliferators and creating opportunities for growth in these new positions. This is like the approach of a wolf pack. By striking fast and hard and fighting on many small fronts, these wolves have a more flexible and fluid response to proliferators using a unified or focused approach.

We saw that Sears wanted to do a wolf-pack strategy by repositioning its mall stores for the women's market, and then creating a pack of specialty stand-alone chains targeting auto parts, home furnishings, and home repair and tools. Sears failed at this because it did not understand how to run the specialty stores. And it failed to recognize the importance of category killers and warehouse formats, so Sears never attacked its competitors in the men's market. Moreover, Sears dedicated too many resources to its mall stores. It suffered from internal conflicts over resources between the powerful managers of the traditional general stores and the less-well-entrenched managers of the upstart stand-alone chains, essentially starving its individual wolves so Sears could not maintain an offensive posture and a healthy wolf pack of its own.

Build Critical Mass

Often firms don't have the critical mass to use different strategies against different proliferators, but they must do so because the market segments are so diverse. Sometimes, players have no choice but to fight on many multiple fronts simultaneously. Firms have to compete as low-cost producers at the low end and as differentiators at the high end of the expected price line, as well as fighting off positions above and below the line. In these cases, companies might directly address the threat of the proliferators by building the mass to field a full portfolio through mergers and acquisitions. Once a full line has been brought together, this strategy requires the deep pockets and managerial talent to sustain a multifronted war.

This was the case in the watch industry. The watch industry is fragmented into many segments that rise and fall as fashion changes. Swatch started out as a focused player—staking out a new position combining low cost and high design—but then went on to create a full portfolio of brands through acquisitions. Swatch initially built its company through inexpensive watches with colorful and unusual designs appealing to fashion forward, younger female consumers. Swatch watches were positioned above the expected price line because they offer a secondary benefit (creative "cool" design and style) above and beyond the primary benefit of watches (prestige). As a result, Swatch could charge a higher price for watches of comparable accuracy, durability, and prestige. But new companies proliferated with new products within Swatch's price segment in different ways. Garmin and Polar, for example, offered hiking watches with GPS positioning and heart-monitoring devices for an added price. Nike offered its unique "just do it" sporty, competitive image and ruggedness for running and other athletic uses. Other firms offered fuller lines of products, such as Citizen, positioned as a line of better prestige watches, while Seiko positioned itself as an even higher prestige line of watches. Dior and Gucci positioned themselves as high prestige fashion watches, while Rolex positioned its product line in the extreme luxury market.

To deal with this proliferation, Swatch Group (formerly SMH) needed greater critical mass if it were to be able to fight on multiple fronts. So Swatch acquired new brands to stake out a full portfolio. In addition to its Swatch brand, the company acquired the line of Blancpain watches, some selling for over $200,000 each; Omega, the watch of astronauts; as well as classic, midrange Hamilton and Tissot watches. It also produces sports and chic watch brands by Longines and Rado. As a company, its diverse products and brands allow it to cover many market segments, selecting from the fully diversified portfolio of watch products to meet anyone, anywhere. Swatch Group is now positioned to change with the changing needs of consumers and the new positioning of rivals, and it has the critical mass to use cross-subsidization from one segment to another.

Time Your Battles

Proliferators can be dealt with sequentially or simultaneously, depending on whether the company has the resources to overwhelm the competition one piece at a time or all at once. In its early days, Microsoft used a sequential strategy to meet and bury many software challengers, incorporating software into Microsoft software before the challengers became killer applications with such wide usage that the challengers could add a Microsoft-like operating system to their killer applications. Microsoft moved from MS-DOS to graphical user interface software (imitating and limiting Apple), to widely used applications such as word processing (eliminating Corel's WordPerfect as a rival), then spreadsheets (eliminating Lotus), and PowerPoint presentation software (eliminating Corel's Presentation), consolidating them all into an office suite.

In one of its later major challenges, Microsoft brutally attacked rival Internet browsers (eliminating Netscape) by bundling its own browser for free with its operating system and allegedly violating antitrust laws when it tried to tie its browser to its operating software to block out rival browsers. Over time, Microsoft has engaged in a sequential series of battles that met, imitated, and absorbed the proliferation of other firms. This expanded Microsoft's business and also helped to discourage potential rivals from invading Microsoft's turf.

Firms can also acquire or absorb threats sequentially or use alliances to make their peace with some potential rivals while keeping others at bay for a limited time (allowing the company to focus on specific threats one at that time). In some cases it is best to deter or delay some threats so you can face them at a later time.

Deter Threats

If the company cannot fight all its threats immediately, it can sometimes neutralize selected threats by scaring off some of the proliferators, thereby freeing up time and resources to focus on more immediate threats. Attacking, buying up, or eliminating proliferators is a very resource-intensive strategy, but sometimes "ghost" products or brands can be used to scare away the proliferators or keep them at bay.

For example, companies scare off rivals by using "ghost products" that exist only in prototype formats to enhance the image of their products and to nullify the image of rivals with better products. Victoria's Secret offers a collection of diamond-studded bras and briefs for price tags of up to $15 million. No one ever buys them—in fact, they are never produced—but this faces down high-end fashion designers that might attack Victoria's Secret by extending into the middle and upper-middle lingerie market. And Microsoft has been accused of using "vaporware" (announced products that do not come to market) to prevent or delay customers from buying a rival's software.

Companies also use *fighting brands*—brands created specifically to attack a rival's key product—to meet proliferators. In the late 1980s, for example, Purina launched a dog food called Graaavy as a direct assault on Quaker's Gravy Train. Purina used the strategy of creating a brand name similar enough to its rival's in order to create confusion in the minds of customers. Purina also priced some of its dry dog food products well below Quaker's to warn Quaker against expanding further into the dry dog food segment. Limiting, scaring off, or buying up some threats can be very important for conserving and focusing resources on the markets of greatest importance to a firm's success.

Turn the Trap to Your Advantage: Outflank the Threats

The final way to meet threats from many sources of proliferation is to turn the proliferation to your advantage by outflanking them with creative proliferation of your own. Threats can be dealt with by finding white space on the map or repositioning to create new growth segments as old ones are saturated.

Fill in the White Space

Firms can counter proliferation by finding new uncontested *white space* along the existing expected price line. For example, restaurants were able to find positions between the quick serve (fast food) and family dining positions on the expected price line, as illustrated in figure 3-5.

FIGURE 3-5

Drilling down on the middle of the expected price line in the restaurant business

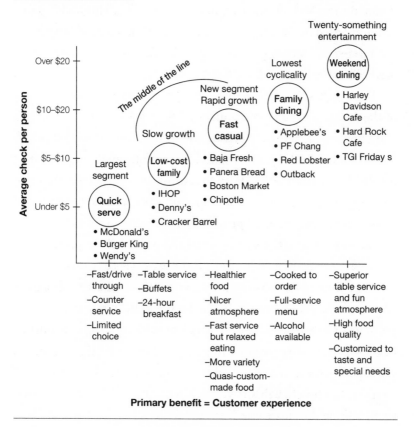

The primary benefit in this case is the customer's satisfaction with the experience they receive while in the restaurant. Satisfaction is created by a combination of the type of service received (counter versus table), food quality (standard products versus customized or healthy), and the atmosphere created. Incremental improvements created new positions along the expected price line. For example, in addition to new positions at the top of the line in the figure (weekend dining), positions have been created between fast-food and family restaurants. One step up from the *quick serve* chains are the *low-cost family* restaurants such as Cracker Barrel, IHOP, and Denny's (some of which repositioned themselves from diners). Then, in the early 2000s, a new segment emerged between low-cost family and family dining, called *fast casual* dining, driven by companies such as Baja Fresh, Panera Bread, Boston Market, and Chipotle Mexican Grill. This middle position was based on healthier food, a nicer atmosphere, and fast service but relaxed eating, more variety, and offerings that were not as standardized as the food found at fast-food restaurants.

This white space can be found by sharpening the understanding of the primary benefit being offered. The primary benefit is often a combination of factors, which can be recombined or altered in different ways to find the white space. By carefully analyzing the combination of factors that made up the customer experience in different types of restaurants, companies can find white space at the high end or low end of the expected price line, or in the middle.

But as we saw in hotels, this white space along the expected price line doesn't remain open for long. If the white space is attractive and there are limited barriers to entry, competitors will arrive shortly—and commoditization begins again. Filling in the white space can be the start of a broader defense strategy of creating a full-line portfolio that acts as a barrier to entry by preemptively filling in all the space across the entire expected price line with blocking brands, as some of the hotel chains have tried with the proliferation of new brands along the entire line.

Create New Segments

If all the white space on the expected price line is filled, the only way to beat proliferation is to create new customer segments above and below the line or to extend the length of the line, as we saw with the lifestyle, designer, and extended-stay brands in hotels. Creating segments requires playing with different secondary benefits, since these secondary benefits can be used to target specific customer groups. The targeted segments are often small niches—witness the hotel industry's efforts to move off the line or to extend it—but this is not necessarily the case.

Las Vegas casinos used different secondary benefits to defend against proliferation in the gambling market created by the threats of new rivals such as Atlantic City, Indian casinos, riverboat casinos, and other venues, as well as the rise of state lotteries, Internet gambling, and upscale international gambling venues in Europe, the Caribbean, the Middle East, and Asia. Vegas has created new customer segments by moving beyond pure and basic gambling to provide weekend entertainment, family vacations, upscale resorts, and adult entertainment in successive waves of new secondary features and services layered on top of their primary benefit—the excitement of risk and potential fortune.

Vegas hotels started as a destination for a diverse set of gamblers. Because the city was the only legal gambling spot in the United States, anyone who wanted to gamble legally had to go to Vegas. Working-class, weekend, inveterate, and vacation gamblers were all part of its customer base. But each new set of competitors forced the Strip to seek new customer segments that had not previously been considered. Some of the ways Vegas continued to identify new customer segments that kept it out of the proliferation trap include:

- *Weekend Gamblers—Gangsters Incorporated:* Vegas hotels were initially a place for local (mainly West Coast) gamblers on weekend trips, attracting a working- or lower-class, inveterate gambling customer base, who liked the "bad-boy" image and excitement of a relatively safe association with the high-profile gangsters who founded Las Vegas.

- *Weekend Entertainment—The Rat Pack Meets Elvis:* Then Vegas became a destination for a wider market seeking not only gambling but also vacations, offering entertainment by the Rat Pack, Elvis, and other stars. Vegas used entertainment, cheap hotel room rates, and inexpensive restaurants to draw people from longer distances. Quickie weddings and divorces were also added to the mix, making Las Vegas the wedding capital of the world. But it also became a place that was often looked on askance because of the type of customer attracted to temporary relationships and a quick buck.

- *Family Vacations and Conventions—Vegas, Vegas, Vegas!:* When Atlantic City casinos entered the market, siphoning off East Coast gamblers seeking the same inexpensive vacation experience and entertainment, Vegas polished up its image. Vegas hotels became family destinations, with full-blown megaresorts (containing attractions such as artificial volcanoes, water parks, pirate ships, zoos, roller-coasters, pyramids, and circuses) to bring in the entire family on vacation and pack the town with conventioneers.

- *Upscale Vacationers and Resort Goers—Euro Vegas:* When Indian and riverboat casinos entered the market, they made weekend gambling accessible on a regional basis—often attracting working-class, senior-citizen, and moderate gamblers. In response, Vegas opened the market for upscale gamblers with resorts such as the Paris, Venetian, and Bellagio Hotels, which offered multimillion-dollar art collections or unique European atmosphere and expensive restaurants and shops. The experience was designed to be like a trip to

Monaco or the French Riviera without the passport. Focus
shifted to the high rollers and their needs, including compli-
mentary concert or show tickets, rooms or meals, personal
valet, maid or chauffeur services, and special rooms.

• *Adult Entertainment—What Happens in Vegas Stays in
Vegas!:* As Internet gambling and high-priced casinos in Asia
and the Middle East closed in on the market, the Strip opened
up a whole new segment that had previously been left to
seedy casinos outside the city limits or off the main Vegas
Strip. In contrast to high tech, it emphasized high-touch, focusing in on the experience and the spectacle that could not
be had on the Internet or in the more prudish foreign locations: sex and a walk on the wild side. Vegas moved to more
adult entertainment, such as more strip shows and racy
nightclub acts. Some hotels paid women to sit at their pools
topless. The pirates of Treasure Island were replaced by the
scantily clad Sexy Sirens of Treasure Island. And, according to
some news reports, some hotels are pushing to legalize prosti-
tution within the city limits of Las Vegas. The target for this
new effort is empty-nesters who no longer have kids at home,
and are looking for a way to live it up and feel young again.[12]

Meanwhile, other casinos tried to cultivate and grow previously
ignored segments. For example, preferential treatment of high
rollers (e.g., shorter lines in restaurants and access to shows) was
commonplace by the 2000s, making it more difficult to target these
"whales," as they are called in the industry. As a consequence, Harrah's introduced its Total Rewards Program, which recognized
highly profitable customers who were *not* high rollers—the frequent
visitors who are slow but steady spenders. In 2003, Harrah's extended the program to allow customers to carry over points from
year to year, so periodic gambler would be recognized for their life-
time value to the casino. As a result, Harrah's share of its customers'

gambling wallet increased from 36 percent in 1998 to 43 percent in 2003. The new benefit offered by Harrah's was no longer defined as the experience within the casino alone, but was defined by an ongoing *relationship* with the casino.

Each of the new moves described above helped Vegas target or create new customer segments and to outflank the competition of the proliferators that entered the market. This process helped the city successfully defeat the threats of a succession of proliferators moving into its turf, retaining its position as one of the largest vacation and convention destination in the world.

New segments can sometimes be identified through leakage analysis, looking at nonusers of the product or service and identifying opportunities to attract these segments as customers. The company can increase customer awareness or overcome bottlenecks such as beliefs and preferences, purchase decisions, and product design problems that might make the offering less attractive to the segment. Companies can also use this type of analysis for current users to identify ways to increase their usage.

Sometimes, it is not enough to use secondary benefits to open new segments. Sometimes companies must reconceptualize the entire market by redefining the primary benefit offered. For example, pharmaceutical companies used to sell directly to doctors but now they increasingly sell their drugs to insurance companies, pharmacy chains, and directly to end consumers, as the power of these other customers has increased during the last two decades. The primary benefit sought by each of these customer segments is different.

For example, doctors are more interested in efficacy and avoiding lawsuits based on side effects, while insurance companies, in order to reduce their future costs, consider cost-efficient prevention of future diseases and drug complications when selecting their formularies. Pharmacy chains are interested in volume discounts and just-in-time inventory management, while most patients just want their disease cured at any price because someone else is usually paying.

In each case, focusing on the new customer segment required new competencies necessary to deliver the new primary benefit required to serve that segment. Moreover, when a new segment is created on the basis of an entirely new primary benefit, the price-benefit analysis typically shows that the proliferation has decreased because most firms will not have the new competencies to deliver on the new primary benefit. So through the lens of the new customer segment, most are not differentiated at all. This type of redefinition can ultimately reset the commoditization process to time zero.

Choose a Threat-Management Strategy

Former General Motors Corporation president and chairman William S. Knudsen once said: "In business, the competition will bite you if you keep running; if you stand still they will swallow you." Ironically for General Motors, its future leaders didn't seem to remember his message. With General Motors' bankruptcy, history has born him out, as proliferating rivals such as Toyota and other foreign rivals transformed the U.S. auto industry, first by focusing on fuel efficiency and reliability and, most recently, on environmentally friendly offerings such as hybrid cars. Proliferation can be used to outflank and avoid threats but also, as shown in the hotel, casino, and auto industries, this proliferation constantly creates new threats for rivals. Threat management is an ongoing process.

The choice of the specific threat-management strategies to meet proliferation depends on the complex balance between a firm's ambitions, resources, and level of threats. Firms' ambitions about their size, scope, and growth are constrained by their finite financial, physical, human, and intangible resources and by external threats varying in danger and attention required. Firms with fewer, less-serious threats and endless resources can pursue wider ambitions, building wider portfolios, breaking up into specialists, and buying up the threats before they get out of hand. But when resources are limited compared with the needs created by the threats, firms resort to avoiding threats and scaling back their ambitions by focusing or sequencing. Or they must resort to confrontation strategies that use fewer resources, such as a using a one-size-fits-all approach, addressing threats sequentially, and deterring or declaring peace with some threats to address others.

The viciousness of the proliferating rivals also affects the choice. Sequential threat elimination may be required if one or two very dangerous proliferators seriously threaten core positions of the firm. And threat avoidance (outflanking) may be required if the proliferators are too vicious to be stopped.

It is important to remember that a firm's resources will constrain a number of strategies for dealing with proliferation, and the feasibility of building products that satisfy new segments may be a critical constraint. For each new segment based on a different type of secondary or primary benefit, managers must ask:

- What obstacles would need to be overcome within my organization?

- What trade-offs between cost and benefits must be overcome?

- Can my firm build or acquire the competencies necessary to deliver the value proposition (benefits and price) needed for the new segment?

- What knowledge about customers and technologies do I need to serve this new segment?

Often, when these questions are answered, there is no feasible white space. If the white space is not there, the company has no choice but to turn and fight.

The logic for balancing resources and threats differs significantly for larger and smaller firms. For larger firms seeking industry leadership, the logic typically follows three general rules:

- *Maximize ambitions*: Firms seeking industry leadership typically want their size and scope to achieve the broadest reach and control over the broadest part of the market, as long as it is profitable. Wide reach is inherent in any attempt to fight off a large number of threats and to move into the growing white spaces as much as possible.

- *Maximize efficient use of resources*: In order to avoid compromising their ambitions, industry leaders try to make the best use of their resources by minimizing the cost of controlling the entire market by skillfully eliminating or preempting the most dangerous proliferators in the most desirable segments.

- *Minimize demands on resources*: To avoid reducing their ambitions, industry leaders also try to minimize the demands on their resources by avoiding, cooperating, and co-opting proliferators in the least desirable segments and by finding cheaper and better offensive strategies—such as scaring off rivals or swallowing them before they consume too much of the leader's energy in unproductive competitive battles.

For smaller firms in an industry, imbalances between the firm's ambitions, resources, and threats will be common. If this is the case, a company typically must decide how to rebalance these elements. The following principles apply:

- *Place resources where they are needed most*: Don't leave critical threats to core markets unchecked. Avoid the threat if it is not affordable to eliminate it, and move resources to the places where the proliferators are biting the hardest if you can win the battle. A company in which resources flow into the core position has greater resources at its center, but faces the threat of starving its peripheral and new positions. The alternative is to have resources flow out of the core in support of the peripheral and new ones, which creates a significant drain on the company's core market and the company's ability to fight off rivals in and around the core.

- *Constrain ambitions:* When threats are too great and conflicts over limited resources are irresolvable, avoid being overstretched by cutting back the firm's scope and focusing resources on the most critical positions in the portfolio.

- *Change the resource needs of different parts of the portfolio*: Done well, the structuring of a company's product or brand portfolio can decrease demands on resources, reduce threats, and increase the efficiency of the use of resources. For example, new positions can be acquired or created to generate resources for the core products. The firm can occupy blocking positions that act as buffers protecting core positions on the price-benefit map, and hence prevent a bloody battle to defend these positions. By careful creation of price-benefit positions that are near or in the core positions of rival firms that act as sporadic thrusts, gambits, and feints—and by fighting judiciously—a company can weaken or keep competitors at bay.

Swings in the overall economy's health also make a big difference. When the economy turns sour, demand will shift to the lower end of the price line (although the very wealthy, except in the most extreme of downturns, will be unaffected, leaving the luxury end of the price line unaffected as well). So firms positioned at the middle and upper-middle of the price line may be hurt, while those at low end may be helped. This will force producers in the middle and upper-middle positions to lower prices, and the low end will be able to raise prices as their demand goes up. The result will be a flattening of the slope of the expected price lines for many firms at the low to middle and even upper-middle positions along the line as the pricing pressure spreads.

For example, as discussed earlier, a shortage of hotel rooms in 2006 and 2007 allowed for a big upward shift in pricing (moving up the expected price line for all firms in the industry), which invited experimentation with new brands and positioning. This shortage of rooms was driven by a very favorable real estate market. But as the real estate market has eroded during the recent economic slump, you would expect to see prices fall back. This could reshape the entire industry by constraining the current degree of experimentation, leading to some consolidation of positions. The rate of these shifts can be measured by watching the changing slope and intercept of the expected price line, allowing firms to observe and forecast how fast they and their rivals might change prices in the market.

Opportunities also affect the choice of threat-management strategies. When price-benefit analysis indicates that there are segments with low competitive intensity, movement to low-intensity positions is possible. However, if the existing positions are saturated with rivals, then filling in the white space above, below, or along the expected price line is advisable and often less risky. When these white spaces appear to be large and highly profitable, firms find it tempting to pursue more risky experiments that might create new segments above and below the expected price line, or open up entirely new markets based on segments that require a new primary benefit. As noted, a depressed economy leads to evaporation of demand, which generally reduces proliferation—but increases deterioration and escalation.

When breaking free of the proliferation trap, it is important to move beyond the traditional resource allocation and budgeting processes employed by most firms. Threat management must be integrated into these processes. In the end, enduring success rests on the ability of managers to recognize the threats and understand the relationship between overstretched resources and ambitions. The financial logic of resource allocation (using internal rate of return and net present value calculations) is not enough to solve the continual challenge of staying in balance. And the financial logic of portfolio analysis used in budgeting processes (such as those based on Boston Consulting Group matrices that move resources from cash cows to growing stars) is also not adequate for confronting the proliferation trap. Only by rebalancing ambitions and threats to fit your resources or by finding ways to make your resources stretch further can you fight off the proliferators without compromising your ambitions for growth and profits.

Once the genie of proliferation is out of the bottle, there is often no putting back the cork. In June 2007, Marriott announced plans to team up with Ian Schrager, the entrepreneur credited with inventing the concept of boutique hotels (such as the Royalton) more than two decades earlier, to create "the first truly global branded boutique lifestyle hotel on a grand scale." The proliferation of adjectives used to describe this new offering is an indication of the complexity of staking out new positions in the modern hotel market. Gone are the days when positions were as distinctive and brilliant as Holiday Inn's great sign. In launching the new boutique chain, Marriott chairman and CEO J. W. Marriott Jr. commented, "We expect the brand to set the standard for decades to come."[13] While such announcements are typically characterized by hyperbole, this is a statement that is unlikely to be true. Even if Marriott does manage to establish a new position that helps the company escape from one proliferation trap, it will not be long before some rival will follow or make its own standard-setting announcement, reshaping positions on the map again.

If you are caught in the middle of a proliferation trap you must remember that "the front is everywhere," as the old maxim of guerilla warfare goes. But four great military geniuses provide the basic guiding principles of fighting on multiple fronts:

- *Antoine-Henri Jomini*: "The party on the defense [must] not divide his forces too much by attempting to cover everywhere."

- *Frederick the Great*: "The first of the two [rivals] who adopts an offensive attitude almost always reduces his rival to the defensive and makes him proceed in consonance with the movements of the former."

- *Sun Tzu*: "He who knows when he can fight and when he cannot will be victorious."

- *Napoleon Bonaparte*: "You must not fight too often with one enemy, or you will teach him all your art of war."

Most firms can't fight everyone, everywhere, all the time. They must try to narrow the front by selecting, outflanking, or overwhelming threats, and they must use their resources wisely by narrowing their fronts, conserving resources using a unified offense, or by building critical mass through acquisition and merger.

FOUR

The Escalation Trap

How to Manage the Escalating Momentum of One-upmanship

Escalation is what happens when companies become locked into a form of one-upmanship—each trying to outdo its rivals by offering the customer more benefits at the same or a lower price. Customers get more and more for their money, and companies lose their margins. This is the escalation trap (see figure 4-1). The dilemma is that no one can be the first to blink. Managers facing escalation can't stand still or they will lose market share to rivals. Meanwhile, engaging in escalation leads to price and benefit wars that cause declining margins and profitability.

The danger signs of an escalation trap are:

- You feel like you are locked into an arms race with competitors, constantly adding new features and benefits and lowering price just to keep up.

FIGURE 4-1

Chapter 4 summary: The escalation trap

	Escalation ↓ Price ↑ Benefits
Description **The causes**	*Escalation:* Caused by rising benefits for the same or lower price. Rivals jockey to offer more value to customers driving competition down toward the lower right-hand corner of the price-benefit map.
Dilemmas **The challenges**	Price-benefit competition can be costly, but no company can afford to be the first to blink and end the game of one-upmanship.
Symptoms **How to identify**	• You are caught up in an arms race • Constantly playing catch-up • Yesterday's competitive advantage is today's entry stakes • Customers are demanding more for less
Solutions **The strategies**	Managing momentum To control the movement of products toward the low price-high benefit corner of the price-benefit map.
Escape the trap	*Re-seize* the momentum.
Destroy the trap	*Reverse* the momentum.
Turn the trap to your advantage	*Harness* the momentum.

- One competitor is making money by leading the escalation of benefits and lowering its costs ahead of price decreases, while you are trapped in a game of nonprofitable catch-up.

- Periodically, you find that the primary benefit—which excited customers yesterday—is taken for granted today and will be no more than entry stakes for tomorrow.

- Your customers have the power to constantly demand more for less money.

As with deterioration, an economic downturn will tend to amplify the effects of escalation. As demand evaporates, customers become more powerful, demanding more for less. Thankfully, there are ways out.

BITTER SWEET: ESCALATION SOURS THE ARTIFICIAL SWEETENER MARKET

We can see the escalation trap at work in the artificial sweeteners market. The introduction of saccharin in 1957 brought such products as Sweet'N Low to our coffee cups. It also brought competition in the market for low-calorie alternatives to sugar. Through a series of innovations, competitors sweetened their value propositions by increasing the primary benefit (sweetness without aftertaste) and reducing price. Sweet'N Low described more than the product.

In addition to the primary benefit of sweetness, newer sweeteners added new secondary benefits that affected pricing included nutrition (especially lower calorie content) and the flexibility of use. These newer sweeteners have different heat stabilities and shelf lives, giving the producers greater flexibility for use in products from carbonated beverages to baking.

At first, saccharin dominated—especially after cyclamates were pulled from the market for safety reasons. Then, in 1981, aspartame was introduced under the NutraSweet and Equal brand names. Aspartame was used for the same purposes as saccharin, but was perceived by customers as higher quality, so it was adopted for use in Diet Coke and Diet Pepsi very soon after its introduction to the market. While aspartame was not quite as sweet at saccharin, it gained wide acceptance because of significantly better safety and taste attributes.

More innovations followed. The first shift in the line occurred in 1988 with the introduction of acesulfame potassium (acesulfame-K, or Ace-K), under the band names Sweet One and Sunnett. While it entered at a lower price point, it was slightly sweeter than aspartame and offered improved secondary benefits, such as better nutritional and flexibility attributes. As a result, aspartame-based products were forced to lower their prices to bring themselves into line with the new competition. NutraSweet gradually cut its price from $90 per

FIGURE 4-2

Escalation in artificial sweeteners*

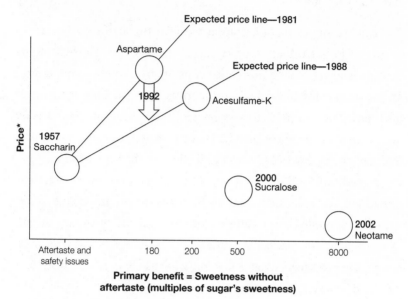

Primary benefit = Sweetness without
aftertaste (multiples of sugar's sweetness)

*Price = Retail price for a sugar-equivalent amount of the sweetener.
**Not to scale.

pound in 1983 to $30 per pound in 1992. So the three products—
saccharin, the reduced-price aspartame, and acesulfame-K—formed
a positively sloped expected price line, with saccharin holding down
the low-priced, low sweetness end of the line and acesulfane-K holding up the high end of the line (see figure 4-2).

But this all changed in 2000. Even though aspartame still held 62
percent of the high-intensity sweetener market, it went off patent at
the end of the 1990s, and sucralose (brand name, Splenda) was introduced in 2000. It was much sweeter than aspartame and also offered improved taste, safety, and heat stability that allowed it to be
used in many new applications, such as baking. Despite these primary and secondary benefits, Splenda entered the market at a lower
price point. Older higher priced–lower quality products remained
on the market owing to switching costs—this was especially true for

large beverage companies, which did not want to risk changing their formulas out of fear of negative customer reactions. Nevertheless, sucralose took 48 percent of the high-intensity tabletop sweetener market by 2004 and expanded into many new uses. This created a negative expected price line. In this instance, some buyers literally pay more for less, an anomaly caused by the switching costs.

Finding the Sweet Spot

Aspartame makers are taking advantage of their overpricing for as long as they can to generate profits and escalate the battle by funding new product development that moves them to the extreme bargain value position (very high sweetness, very low price). New products include neotame (eight thousand times as sweet as sugar) for baking and cultured products, as well as a blend of aspartame and acesulfame-K (branded Twinsweet) that achieves a taste similar to sugar when used along with high-fructose corn syrup.

As the pattern of escalation of benefits at lower prices in this market continues to play itself out, players are trying to break out of the cycle before they bottom out at the low price–high benefit position—the "ultimate value point" in the eyes of customers. My research found that the primary solutions to this escalation trap involve managing momentum, controlling the progress of this competitive escalation, or re-seizing the momentum.

Sweetener manufacturers, for example, are working to re-seize the momentum. Some companies are changing the primary benefit, moving from sweetness (a property of the product) to creating solutions for food companies. For example, this might include creating blends and new sweeteners that enable food companies to offer low-carbohydrate baked products with long shelf lives that previously were impossible or not very tasty.[1] And companies are looking at other solutions, such as flavor and nutrient additives, that might allow them to offer a much wider selection of solutions to food companies developing new products.

PRIMO BATTLES THE ESCALATION TRAP

So what can managers caught in the escalation trap do about it? The first step is to realize that you are in the trap. If you don't figure out how to manage a battle of one-upmanship, you are liable to lock yourself into an endless, fruitless arms race.

Primo, a $1 billion division of a *Fortune* 500 U.S. company, appeared to be in a good position when I began working with managers there in 1997.[2] It was the industry leader in its market for a high-tech material used in components purchased by numerous consumer, business, and industrial electronics manufacturers. But an unseen and unacknowledged threat lurked: Primo was facing commoditization. Fierce international competition had decreased prices and increased benefits for customers. The Primo leadership team was partly in denial and partly handicapped by not having an accurate picture of the market. Working together, we sought to understand how the price and benefit positions were evolving in its industry. Primo ultimately used these insights to turn the tables on competitors.

Primo Pricing

Primo's story is salutary. The company offered a differentiated premium-priced product with better performance compared with its major rivals—including the U.S. company Neutryno and two Japanese competitors: TokyoTech and Samur-Ion. To gain share, the competitors differentiated themselves at first. Some boasted of fewer defects, others of multiple sizes and materials tailored to specific uses. Then these features became standard. Everyone offered a similar material that was rarely defective and useful for all sizes and major purposes. As a result, these attributes were no longer what determined the price.

Pricing pressure intensified as previous product benefits commoditized, but Primo still thought it was sitting pretty. After all, it dominated the high end of the line—the best-performing materials in the market, which was still the most profitable segment. Although Primo had the largest market share, its managers knew that rivals were engaged in raising benefits and reducing costs. What they didn't know was how fast this competition might escalate and what it might mean to Primo. Based on historic rates, Primo managers and I projected the trajectories of rivals over the next two years. This yielded an important insight: the trends would ultimately give Primo's competitors considerably more market share because they would soon be offering more for less at the low and middle segments of the market.

Primo's managers were very concerned. I asked them: What would happen to the industry if this trajectory continued? Given that Primo couldn't freeze the industry in place, what could Primo do about this?

When Primo managers looked at the projected historical trajectories, they realized the picture was not pretty. They anticipated that in two years a *new* expected price line would be established. With the emergence of this new line, Primo at best would sustain its current position at the top end of the line and hold on to its current market share because of customer loyalties. But customers were fickle, so the more likely scenario was that Primo's high-end position would lose share to the low-end players for two reasons:

- *The lure of more value:* Trends showed that the low-end players would increase the value they offered to customers relative to Primo's high-end offering. The projected price line's slope was getting steeper—meaning that the benefit-to-price ratio was increasing at the low end of the line.

- *The inertia of sufficient value:* Because the projected low end was not as low as it had been two years previously (low-end rivals were creeping up), Primo could foresee erosion of its market share if customers were willing to settle for a good-enough level of benefit at a lower price.

This escalation posed a dilemma for Primo: because it had the largest market share, it had the most to lose from price reductions. Even if it retained its position at the top end of the line without loss of market share, the company would likely see its margins eroded because it would have to offer high-end products at lower prices than it did two years previously. But if it didn't act, it could lose market share rapidly and ultimately might have to concede its market leadership. Primo couldn't afford to stand still, but it also couldn't merely follow competitors. Primo's managers worried: Could they escape this trap?

Taking the Lead

Primo's managers developed a plan to lead the way, outflank, and preempt competitors. Instead of stopping the escalation, they decided to lead it. Primo first moved at the high end, pushing the expected price line to much higher levels of the primary benefit and slightly lower prices. It did so by increasing investment in R&D to create several process and product breakthroughs that allowed the company to lower its manufacturing costs and raise product performance. And Primo split its high-end position into three products so that some of the customers looking for middle-level benefit might move up and abandon competitors' products, while the highest-end customers might be enticed to stick with premium-priced products a little longer. Overall, Primo's margins did not erode very much because these actions counterbalanced each other (see figure 4-3).

Primo's rivals were taken by surprise. They had continued to lower their costs and boost performance at their historic rates, but Primo's actions resulted in tilting the expected price line in Primo's favor. A flatter expected price line meant the high-end products now offered better value to customers (i.e., an improved performance to price ratio) relative to the low-end products. So Primo gained share compared with the low-end products, more than making up for the

FIGURE 4-3

Primo takes control by setting the pace of escalation

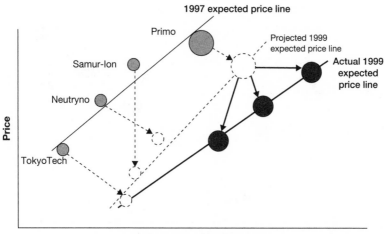

Primary benefit = Performance

Price index = Price per unit of performance. Grey circle size = Actual 1997 market share and position; dotted circles are projected 1999 positions; black circles are Primo's actual position and share in 1999 and 2000.

small amount it lost in margins. The U.S. rival, Neutryno, was badly hurt. Its middle-level product was almost wiped out by Primo's higher-performance, lower-priced, midlevel product.

There was another benefit from this strategy. Because Primo had lowered price and raised performance, demand grew. Its products were more affordable, so the customer base and usage expanded. But that was not enough for Primo. Using the revenue from its successful high-end business, it invested to move even more aggressively against its rivals. In 2000, Primo stopped them in their tracks by moving down its new expected price line to a low-cost position at the basic end of the market (see figure 4-4). By doing so, Primo stopped Japanese rivals from further commoditizing the market, weakening both rivals and leaving them without the R&D funds to continue to race toward the lower right of the diagram at the same rate. This slowed the escalation for the next few years, trapped the

FIGURE 4-4

**Primo attacks the low end and positions for the future
at the high end**

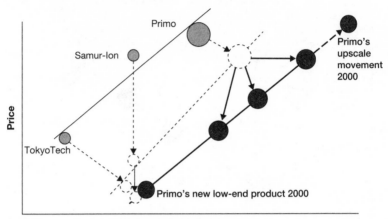

Primo

Samur-Ion

Primo's
upscale
movement
2000

Price

TokyoTech

Primo's new low-end product 2000

Primary benefit = Performance

Price index = Price per unit of performance. Grey circle size = Actual 1997 market share and position;
dotted circles are projected 1999 positions; black circles are Primo's actual position and share in 1999
and 2000.

Japanese in an undesirable segment of the market, and ultimately
forced U.S.-based Neutryno to exit the market. Plus it bought Primo
time to begin its next big move.

Primo did not stand still. It built on its momentum by investing
in R&D to introduce a new, very high-end product in late 2000 for
use in cutting-edge components that would be the foundation of
the next generation of products coming onto the market. Primo
reduced the price of this high-end product from 2001 to 2004 as it
gained experience and economies of scale in production, moving
the product from a high-end niche to a mass-produced product. Finally, Primo milked some of its old product line to subsidize the for-
mation of a new product line and a new expected price line by 2004.
Post-2004, Primo continued to extend its product line into higher-
margin, higher-performance products while the Japanese struggled
at the low end. Because Primo continued its pressure on Japanese
competitors by pinning them down at the low end, its rivals were

FIGURE 4-5

Cornering the market, 2001–2005

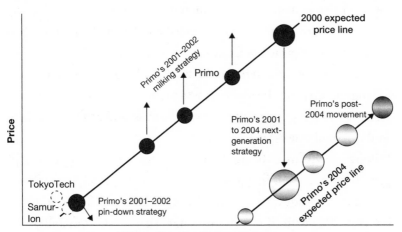

Price index = Price per unit of performance. Black circles are Primo's products in 2000; shaded grey circles are Primo's products in 2004 and beyond.

not only trapped in their current segment of the market by 2001, but they were still playing catch-up four years later (see figure 4-5).

By 2000, Primo had not only escaped the escalation trap, it had turned the tables on its rivals, outpacing them at the low end, cutting off their low-end movement, and leaving them out flanked. These rivals were facing their own escalation trap. Indeed, the Japanese competitors would have been crushed were it not for the deep pockets of their parent companies, which were willing to sustain substantial losses and subsidize them over the long term.

Primo harnessed the escalation process and shifted the entire expected price line, expanding the range of performance to new heights. By quantifying and seeing the rate and direction of competitive moves and the consequent shifts in the expected price line, Primo was able to develop a creative strategy with more precise price and benefit targets as it moved in increments. And by mapping the price and benefit movement over several time periods, Primo was also able to see the big trends in how the expected price line was moving, finding a way out of its trap by outpacing its rivals and controlling their movement. Primo harnessed the momentum, escalating the price-benefit war faster than others could keep up, leading the way to lower-price and higher-benefit positions and then reshaping the expected price line.

Not every solution to the problem of escalation creates a problem for competitors, but the idea here was to find a way out of the trap by pushing the competitors into a low end corner and positioning them so they could not escape by escalating even further. This prevented Primo's growth from being illusory or temporary, as so often happens as rivals are left in a position to continue to catch up and then neutralize any advantage of the leader. Primo is still the industry leader in 2009 with commanding market share and profitability.

COMMODITY DELL . . . OR COMMODITY HELL?

As another example of escalating price-benefit wars, consider the computer industry. In 2000, the industry appeared to be imprisoned in an escalation trap created by Dell, but rivals ultimately found ways to escape.

Dell developed a model to deliver high-quality, customer-designed, low-cost computers directly to consumer and business clients, driving down costs and squeezing margins across the industry. Prices fell to incredible levels and Dell appeared to be unstoppable. Given this escalation of the price and benefits war, competitors such as Hewlett-Packard and IBM found it increasingly difficult to compete against Dell in the PC business.

Both HP and IBM found different paths out of this trap. Hewlett-Packard chose to gain the scale and new technologies it needed to compete. Despite internal resistance and bumpy integration issues, HP's acquisition of Compaq ultimately gave it the scale and technology needed to radically differentiate its products and make HP the market leader. IBM took a different approach, selling its personal computer business to the even lower low-cost Chinese manufacturer Lenovo. This allowed IBM to concentrate more on its tech solutions business and other high-end, differentiated computer products and services, exiting the low-margin PC business. IBM didn't just exit; it created a killer, even lower-cost competitor for Dell at the same time.

Suddenly, Dell found itself in a commodity trap. Proliferation trapped Dell between HP and Lenovo. Dell's position was also undermined by the proliferation of low-cost laptops. While Dell's PCs could be customized with an array of different components, laptops integrated screens, keyboards, and other features into standard low-cost bundles, making Dell's customization less valuable. Dell found itself facing commoditization of its desktops by proliferating products attacking from above (HP), below (Lenovo), and from the sides (laptops from diverse manufacturers). The net effect of both HP's and IBM's actions was to stop Dell's momentum by creating a proliferation trap.

In other cases, firms proactively drive growth (rather than margins) to create shareholder value. They do so by escalating the price-benefit war so fast that they lead the pack and cause a large shakeout in the market. For example, Hewlett-Packard drove down the cost of printing technology to take color printing from a small luxury niche to a mass market. It used ink-jet technology to redefine the value proposition for color copies, offering a machine for $2,500 that produced results comparable to a $20,000 professional color copier. Then it continued to shift the decimal point on its printer prices and boost quality, to the point that the company often gives away low-end printers with the purchase of a PC. The cost of color copies went from the $1 or $1.50 per page charged by copy centers to about 7 cents per page or less. This shift opened up the market to home offices, small businesses, and amateur digital photography. It was one of the reasons that HP came to dominate the printer market. HP also changed the business and pricing model in the industry, practically giving away printers while making money on expensive ink cartridges. This helped to lower the prices of equipment and to stimulate growth. It now has such scale and technology advantages that HP practically owns the market, with significant barriers to entry for others.

STRATEGIES FOR RESPONDING TO ESCALATION

There are many variations of this escalation trap and the strategies for beating it, but all involve managing the momentum of escalation—by reversing, harnessing, or re-seizing the momentum. In the following examples, I will consider momentum management strategies for dealing with the escalation trap in more detail.

Escape the Trap: Re-seize the Momentum

Escalation can ultimately give way to a more radical change: the momentum it creates can cause the market to metamorphose to a completely different primary benefit or product offering. The music-oriented iPod morphed into the iPhone and videogame players, for example. Similarly, artificial sweetener makers morphed into solution providers; GE turbines into service providers; and military night-vision goggles into integrated battlefield command-and-control systems. The other two strategies discussed below—harnessing and freezing momentum—both have limited efficacy; eventually a company must re-seize the momentum with a momentous move. This is the most effective way to escape from the escalation trap

My research on the small-car segment of the automobile market revealed that the U.S. manufacturers could not reverse the escalating price-benefits wars driven by some Asian competitors during the 1990s. Instead, they had to resort to frequent redefinitions of the primary benefit driving prices. When there is rapid imitation and aggressive competitive behavior, the primary driver of price shifts constantly as old primary benefits become less valuable and new primary benefits are needed to replace them. More frequent redesign and retooling is necessary. To escape, firms need to anticipate or drive the shifts rather than fall victim to them by playing constant catch up.[3]

In the case of small cars, in 1993 the primary benefit was *platform*, a combination of features indicating the vehicle's size, including the number of passengers, the chassis size, and the trunk and gas tank capacity, the crashworthiness of the vehicle, the engine power, and its gas usage. By 1995 emphasis had switched to *Consumer Reports'* endorsement emphasizing reliability, in particular the defect rate and cost of repairs while under warranty during the first year. Then the primary benefit shifted to antilock brakes (safety) in 1999.

Viewing this history, I discovered a rhythm of change. Changes in primary benefits appeared to run in three- to four-year cycles. Thus, using price-benefit analysis at several points in time can help firms know when and how to shift their R&D to focus on the most important emerging benefit and to establish the "Moore's law" of their industry.[4]

Different industries are likely to have different rhythms. For example, gasoline stations have redefined the primary benefit they offer at regular ten-year intervals to serve different needs:

- *In the 1960s:* They were *full service stations*, offering mechanics, window washing, and high-performance gas to serve the needs of muscle cars, total car care, and the desire for personal service from a trusted source.

- *In the 1970s:* They became *self-service filling stations*, offering do-it-yourself pumps with choices of unleaded and diesel fuel in many new locations to serve the needs created by the energy crisis, a more on-the-go lifestyle, as well as offering assurance of not being stranded without gas.

- *In the 1980s:* They became *convenience stores* using gas and automated car washes as lures to bring people into a retail store. The goals were to serve the needs of people whose longer work days and commutes created the need for fast one-stop shopping.

- *In the 1990s:* They converted to *safe and secure havens*, serving the needs of lone women for improved safety and security during extended hours by offering faster ways to pay (e.g., speed passes and credit card pumps) coupled with better lighting and security cameras for nighttime purchasers.

- *In the 2000s:* They converted their retailing from small convenience store selections to a much broader array of merchandise and services, including alliances with Dunkin' Donuts and high-end coffee retailers.

- *In the future:* Many believe gas stations will morph into green centers for alternative fuels, such as electricity for hybrid cars and water for hydrogen cars.

The gas station example points out another major way to anticipate the timing of redefinitions of the primary benefit that must be offered: watch changing customer needs and demographics. Shifts in the importance of different benefits are driven by changes in customers as well as competitors. In the gas station case, the changes in primary benefit occurred as responses to shifts in customer needs as people changed their work and life patterns, as well as their price sensitivities during glut and shortage periods.

Or consider the approximately five-year rhythms in the property and casualty insurance industry. The market leaders in insurance sequentially redefined the primary benefit four times over approximately two decades to avoid commoditization caused by escalation. When primary benefits became standard and low priced, the industry moved on and established new primary benefits. Insurers moved from one primary benefit to another:

- First, emphasizing financial strength (guaranteeing payout reliability)

- Second, providing diverse services (such as getting quick rate quotes or faster claims processing) and bundled products including car, home, boat, summer home, motorcycle, RV, and other types of property and casualty insurances

- Third, offering value pricing

- Fourth, offering specialty value positions targeted at specific low-risk niches

And now firms such as Geico are emphasizing branding and new distribution channels. Geico is using direct selling online and via the mail to bypass high-cost agents, as well as clever and memorable ads: for example, the ads using the Geico gecko to build name recognition and the ads pushing online distribution by claiming "even a caveman can do it." The company's strategy appears to be paying off. In January 2009, at a time when other insurance companies were announcing layoffs, Geico announced it was actively recruiting new staff.

To support successive redefinitions of the primary benefit, insurance companies had to preplan and gradually build the creation of new know-how and competencies to ensure delivery of each new primary benefit before the next inflection point of change. For example, an emphasis on financial strength required effective balance sheet management. When focus shifted to diverse services and products, a larger number of insurance agents was required. Value pricing required economies of scale and lower costs in operations and overhead through automation using IT, while in the next stage, insurers found specialty value propositions involving new pricing schemes.

Using deeper data mining, insurance company Allstate developed a sophisticated pricing model. Instead of grouping customers into three broad categories, Allstate identified more than fifteen hundred different customer categories, allowing it to match premiums more closely to risk. This new "tiered pricing" strategy meant that the company could offer lower premiums to safer drivers while still keeping claims expenses down. After implementing the new system, Allstate's operating income rose 16 percent and its return on equity hit 15 percent.

Auto insurer Progressive has also redefined pricing for auto insurance by offering customers side-by-side comparisons of its prices with competitors, instead of just quoting customers its own premiums. It even tried to offer policies with usage fees that charged drivers by the number of miles they drove.

In all three industries (small cars, gas stations, and insurance), each shift in the primary benefit brought the entire industry along with it, forcing laggards to catch up by adding the new benefits that became the new basis of competition, rather than establishing new niches. Those who didn't keep up with these rhythmic cycles were forced to fight using price to make up for their deficiencies, and most of these laggards died off or were bought up.

Set the Pace

When re-seizing the momentum, it is often best to pace and prepare for the shifts because it is not easy to build new know-how and core competencies on a just-in-time basis. Waiting until competitors have shifted may be too late, forcing laggards into a losing game of constant catch-up. So the ability to periodically re-seize the momentum necessitates a set of new capabilities.

What are the capabilities that companies need to successfully pace and prepare for periodic re-seizing of the momentum? Successful pacesetters are good at managing transitions, so that they can move quickly and smoothly to each new primary benefit. They develop the capabilities for future primary benefits before the previous one runs out of steam and erodes. In essence, to be good at pacing means managing four simultaneous separate and parallel organizations within the firm. These organizations are responsible for four tasks:

- *Doing:* The first organization is operationalizing the current primary benefit, doing the routine actions of manufacturing and selling today's primary benefit.

- *Setting up:* The next organization is setting up the organization, plant, and distribution needed to sell an already-developed next-generation product with the new primary benefit that is waiting in the wings for the right moment to be introduced.

- *Planning:* The third organization is researching changes in the customer and technology markets and developing the people, competencies, technologies, and products that drive or support the third-generation primary benefit.

- *Envisioning:* The fourth organization is thinking broadly about what might come next and investing resources in researching the implications of long-term trends, basic technical research, and early prototyping for distant potential definitions of the primary benefits that may become important to success.

To be effective at pacing and preparing for periodic re-seizures of the momentum, organizations need to do each of these four tasks well, and at the same time. This usually means giving each task its own people, budget, and facilities. There must be clear processes for rotating people out of one organization to the next and retraining people for the next primary benefit so that there are always people who understand the firm's capabilities in these different stages of development and who are ready to participate in building future capabilities. While some organizations may look toward megatrends in society, economics, demographics, and other macro changes to help set the pace of shifts in primary benefits, the challenge is to determine which primary benefits to be developing for the future. Price-benefit analysis can also help firms target the right benefits for development by watching which are rising and which are falling in importance as price drivers.

To force the firm to proactively set the pace, organizations often set strict timetables for the transition from one primary benefit to the next, using milestones and budgets that force forward movement. Some companies use planning processes to drive re-seizures. Other companies use strong performance metrics and goals (such as the percentage of revenues that must come from new products each year) that focus the organization on time pacing. This internal process of thinking ahead to the next cycle of primary advantage is critical in driving the type of external pacing discussed in the gasoline station and insurance company examples. The aim is to identify the rhythmic periods so that a firm can set timetables and milestones for doing, setting up, planning, and envisioning that will preempt rivals.

There is also an art to making the handoff from one primary benefit to the next. Kathleen Eisenhardt and Shona Brown compare this to a relay race in which the handoff of the baton is often as important to success as the speed of the individual runners.[5] Companies that are effective at pacing manage these handoffs by matching their internal rhythms to the changes in the market and synchronizing them with the actions of suppliers and other partners. Successful companies also create capabilities and processes that allow them to cannibalize themselves, providing the culture and incentives necessary for motivating employees supporting the previous primary benefit to give up their businesses, share their knowledge and resources, and to support the new one without hindering its progress.

One challenge for the company re-seizing the momentum is to gauge when the ultimate value point is reached—where there is little or no opportunity to push prices lower, improve upon the primary benefit, or expand the market. This is when harnessing the momentum of the last primary benefit must give way to re-seizing the momentum using a new primary benefit. The leader needs to be prepared to redefine the primary benefit in some way to re-seize the momentum, or to move to a strategy of slowing or reversing the momentum. So it is important to monitor the price-benefit equation to understand and predict the shifts in the primary benefit. Managing this pacing requires that companies are just fast enough to stay ahead of competition but not faster, to avoid jumping too soon and throwing margins away. Among the capabilities needed for effective timing of these shifts are competitive intelligence and marketing skills that extend the current primary benefit as long as possible, as well as the capabilities to launch quickly and reduce the risks of launching products based on new primary benefits.

Destroy the Trap: Reverse the Momentum

Re-seizing the momentum is one way to escape the escalation trap. But there are other ways to attack it. The second strategy involves trying to slow or even reverse the momentum. This can restore balance to the industry and prevent further erosion of price. This is particularly important if cost-reducing, benefit-improving innovations are not available or if the market is not price or benefit sensitive so that growth cannot be stimulated by lowering prices or raising benefits. In this case, the goal is, as much as possible, to hold back or reverse the escalation.

Freeze Positions

Think back to the heavy industries of yesteryear. My research led me to the market for turbine power generators in the 1960s. At that time, GE held the large turbine market. It focused on larger, leading-edge turbines for major private-sector utilities, because they were not very price sensitive, made up two-thirds of the demand, and offered higher growth rates and much higher margins than small turbines. This position left GE's arch rival, Westinghouse, to serve small municipal utilities and government utilities that typically sought public bids. GE blocked Westinghouse out of the large-turbine market using economies of scale, superior technology, and prices that were below Westinghouse's costs.

GE also dealt with Westinghouse by containing its rival in small-turbine segments. GE encouraged Westinghouse to stay out of large turbines by staking out a minor toehold position in the smaller-turbine market and offering its products at a higher price than Westinghouse. This allowed GE to shape the slope of the expected price line by setting a price ceiling on what Westinghouse could charge at the low end of the market. GE was positioned to lower its prices in small turbines to discipline Westinghouse if it expanded into the large-turbine segment. And GE was positioned to set the prices at the high end because its superior technology and lower costs from its economies of scale in technology and manufacturing allowed GE to price below Westinghouse's costs if need be.

To further strengthen its position, GE purchased some commodity inputs from Westinghouse, as well as licensing some technology to Westinghouse for use in the low-end market. This made Westinghouse more profitable but also more dependent on GE. Often, using published price lists, GE signaled its prices in both segments to encourage Westinghouse to follow its leadership in the market. The idea was to prevent Westinghouse from price discounting during bad times, instead providing a win-win for both firms if Westinghouse would follow GE's signals to raise prices. But when this process became too obvious, it generated some serious government scrutiny over antitrust concerns. Even so, the relationship between Westinghouse and GE persisted legally from the 1950s to the 1990s, until Westinghouse was acquired by Siemens. With Siemens now at the party, price and benefit competition—that is, escalation—restarted because Siemens had new technologies and deep pockets. GE was forced to change what it offered by transforming the primary benefit away from the product's technologies to services, including financing, preventative maintenance, and outsourcing services that minimized the customers' risk of generator failures. As of 2008 Siemens is trying to provide similar services, but GE's manufacturing operations are better located and staffed for serving the U.S. market, which is still the largest user of energy in the world.

Companies also can dampen escalation by locking customers into long-term contracts, using high switching costs or other strategies that ensure brand loyalty, market share, and prices. One example is the carbon black market (a chemical used in tires, inks, and other products). Carbon black is a small but critical part of tires—it gives the rubber in tires its firmness and strength—so tire makers cannot afford a shortage that would hold up production, and are thus willing to lock themselves into contracts that span several years.

One of the market leaders in the industry, Cabot Corporation, has used long-term contracts, when possible, to lock in customers. Customers will typically agree to these contracts when there are concerns about shortages of quality supply. Shipping distances mean that there are lag times between a shortage and its impact on auto production rates, which makes locking in supplies more important. Automakers are less concerned about driving down prices of carbon black than they are about ensuring supply and avoiding the cost of idle plants. Long-term contracts such as these, as well as other strategies for locking-in customers, can dampen the escalation that might lead to price wars and other challenges.

The competition between firms positioned in different places along the expected price line can also be muted by using careful positioning to effectively divide up the market. Different quality grades of carbon black affect performance—the primary benefit offered—so differences in product grades can secure a firm's position at the most profitable places along the expected price line. As Ken Burnes, Cabot's chairman, president, and CEO, told me:

> *In the market for carbon black, we have been the technical leader. Competitors continually match or erode away our differentiation, and the only effective defense is to the keep improving the quality and performance of our products, to continue to tweak the product to hold our value for the customer. We have taken stronger positions with higher cost grades and ceded some of the lower cost grades to other competitors. Each competitor's technology has a sweet spot in the market, creating products with different functionality or used for different purposes. We have to constantly develop and defend our sweet spot.*[6]

While a technological advantage might be used to drive escalation (as in Primo's case), Cabot's focus on specific "sweet spots" and "tweaking to hold value," as well as the use of long-term contracts, stops potential escalation in a commodity market. To the extent that competitors are focused on different positions along the expected price line, they avoid going head-to-head with one another, and this creates a more stable environment, reducing the temptation to engage in escalation.

Raise the Bar

Instead of freezing the players' positions in different places on the line, companies can also elevate the entire line for the industry (or a segment). This tends to dampen—or even reverse—escalation because prices go up across the board. As part of a project for a major carmaker, we discovered that this elevation of the line occurred when we calculated the expected price line for sports and sporty cars in 1993 and 1999.

Before this time, the movement in the market was quite different. Japanese carmakers were escalating the competition in this segment with the introduction of highly reliable, lower-priced sports cars like the Mazda Miata and the Nissan 280Z.

Even though these Japanese cars were successful, as one might expect, sports car buyers as a whole are not like other car buyers. It was no surprise that our analysis revealed that the primary benefit of sports and sporty cars offered in the United States was performance. Performance was measured using the engine power divided by the vehicle chassis size, an indicator of the car's "pep," including its acceleration rate and maximum speed of the vehicle.

Two other benefits contributed to sports car prices in 1993: the car's platform and reliability. But both declined in importance from 1993 to 1999, and reliability even stopped being a factor in determining price by 1999, since all the competitors had improved their reliability. This eliminated the appeal of the Japanese models, making it easier for rivals to regain control over pricing—that is, to elevate the expected price line.

The presence of antilock brakes, safety (results in crash tests, and the presence of air bags), and the *Consumer Reports* overall rating of the vehicle did not affect prices, even though these were significant in other segments of the automobile market. As you can imagine, sports car enthusiasts are not terribly interested in safety or the conservative, penny-pinching *Consumer Reports* ratings. They are interested in speed and are willing to pay for it. During this period there was no redefinition of the primary benefit in the market—performance was consistently the most important price driver, and prices for different levels of performance were going up as the industry's expected price line moved upward on the price-benefit map.

This price-benefit analysis and the elevation of the expected price line give important data about the nature of competition in this segment, suggesting that escalation can be prevented and even reversed. Unlike more price-sensitive segments of the market where advances in performance might lead to limited price increases, or even price reductions, this segment is able to charge a premium for these advances, and pricing actions can avoid or reverse escalation. In addition, R&D can be directed toward improving performance and platforms to increase prices, without too much attention paid to other secondary benefits because the determinants of sports car prices do not shift a lot from year to year.

Reversing the momentum was possible in the sports car market for several reasons. The segment is characterized mostly by price-in-sensitive consumers and several niche brands that prefer margins over volume. Moreover, barriers to entry are rather high due to the challenge of acquiring technology, service networks, a high-status image, and reputation in this market, which often involves large investments and sustained success at high-profile racing events. Consistent with this notion is the fact that sports cars were the only market segment of the automobile industry to see the number of competing models reduced (by three) from 1993 to 1999. As a result, the market segment is dominated by a few, high-labor-cost (mostly European) manufacturers, which further reduces the motivation of incumbents to break away from high prices or to redefine the primary benefit offered by sports cars.

Turn the Trap to Your Advantage: Harness the Momentum

The third approach to escalation is to use the momentum to drive and control escalation, forcing others to race to keep up, as Primo did in the first round of its competition with Japanese rivals (see figure 4-3). In the high-tech business of military night-vision goggles, ITT used momentum to drive escalation. Steve Loranger, CEO of ITT Industries, told me how his company has harnessed commoditization by lowering prices, improving performance, and expanding the market: "We offer a thousand times the power with less than half the weight and size for half of the price, and have stimulated an explosion in demand, making night vision standard issue for the U.S. military. As we get more innovative and leverage our scale, we are able to offer even lower prices and our operating margins are going up."[7]

Think of it: a thousand times the power at half the price, yet margins are going up! It is perhaps counterintuitive, but harnessing escalation is a powerful way to use the momentum of price-benefit warfare. This is especially shocking when you consider that some of the most popular and standard models of strategy advise that you should not escalate rivalry, but actively work to reduce the rivalry within the industry.

Think again. If harnessed, a decline in pricing grows the market. As the technology moves from use by military specialists to standard issue for almost every GI, it means the market can profitably support higher quality at a lower price. The secret to making escalation work is to relentlessly reduce your own costs before reducing your prices, while forcing rivals to lower price and then catch up on cost reductions.

But there is a limit to how far this can go. At a certain point when all soldiers have its night-vision technology, ITT will need to redefine the primary benefit offered by its product in order to restart the escalation along a new benefit dimension. For example, ITT's next move is to tie its night-vision systems into its GPS, mapping, and communications systems so that commanders and soldiers have a full, real-time picture of the battlefield and know where the "friendlies" and enemies are. Eventually, the primary benefit of night-vision systems might not be night vision, but a new type of vision that only an integrated battlefield communications system can provide. Harnessing the momentum generally gives way to re-seizing the momentum. In the meantime (and this may last for years), ITT has led the market and built its business by harnessing the momentum of escalation based on the current primary benefit of better sight in the dark.

Roll the Apples

Apple has also harnessed the momentum of escalation in launching successive generations of iPods, reducing price and increasing the primary benefit for the entire line with each successive generation.

(The primary benefit in this case is multifaceted functionality combining numerous sources, including storage, software, content, sleek design, and features—all of which contribute to the iPod's image of providing an easy-to-use, cutting-edge product.) Apple has drawn its line and then redrawn it in ways that force competitors to keep racing to catch up (see figure 4-6).

In July 2002, Apple introduced the first iPods, 5- and 10GB (gigabyte) digital devices for music storage and playback, enabling novel features such as playlists, digital libraries, and music groups. In July 2003, Apple lowered the price and extended the line, but made the devices even more functional by opening the iTunes online music store, selling legally downloadable songs for the iPod.[8] Responding to low-end entries by Sony, Dell, and Creative Technology in January 2004, Apple lowered its price per gigabyte on the low end of its line, and also introduced the 4GB Mini to take advantage of rivals' lack of sleekness, as well as the Photo to enhance capacity for digital photos. In February of 2005, Apple pushed the low end lower with the Shuffle to block entry by low-cost imitators, and then the super-slim Nano, the width of six stacked credit cards. The company now had a full line of traditional iPods in place to block entry by would-be rivals at any point from low- to high-end devices.

Apple became the dominant player in digital music and continued to expand with the growing market. After introducing the iPod, Apple recognized that escalation would occur—more benefits would be offered for the same or lower prices. But Apple didn't try to stop this escalation; instead, it harnessed the momentum and drove it. In this way it deterred a flood of entrants that might have tried to imitate the iPod. Apple actually *shortened the intervals* between shifting expected price lines of products, setting an accelerating pace that made it difficult for rivals to catch up.

Notice that each time Apple appears to reach the bottom of this process (the lower right of the diagram), it adds new capabilities.

FIGURE 4-6

iPod uses the momentum of escalation

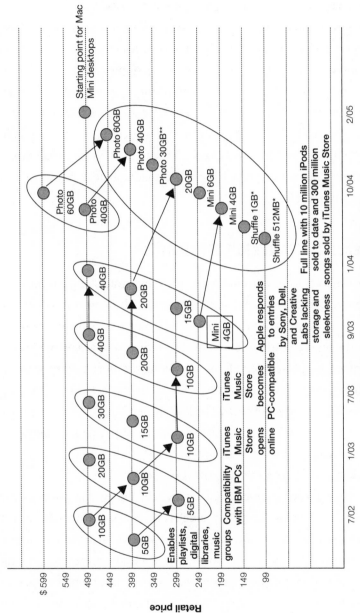

Primary benefit = Cutting-edge functionality

*First iPods with flash memory to reduce weight and cost.

**iPod Photo models process digital photos as well as music.

This extends the market further and further to the right, keeping the process alive. For example, it has added new capabilities to increase the "coolness" of its products by making them video capable and offering new content such as downloads of videogames as well as *Lost*, *Desperate Housewives*, and other network television shows through its online store. And, in the ultimate move, Apple added wireless connectivity, voice telephony, and a fully functional Internet browser to redefine its devices completely. The iPod metamorphosed into two new products: the iPhone and a color-screen videogame player. So Apple keeps finding ways to continue to harness the momentum, and then proactively re-seizing the initiative before others take it away from Apple.

CHOOSING A MOMENTUM STRATEGY

If the market can be stimulated to grow by endless opportunities to improve benefits or lower costs, it can be advantageous to harness the momentum to drive escalation. But to be successful at this strategy, the market leader must be able to reduce its costs before lowering price so it can profit all the way along the escalation process. In contrast, the follower company is forced to play catch-up, dropping prices before reducing costs. The leader then builds up momentum, forcing everyone else to catch up, stimulating growth in demand, encouraging a shakeout of weak rivals, and playing a game of chicken that scares away even the most powerful rivals.

While harnessing escalation can benefit the leading company for years, this process ultimately accelerates the movement toward a position of *ultimate value* (from the customers' perspective) where customers get a great deal, but almost all advantage and pricing power—and margins—are competed away. At this point, companies need to redefine the primary benefit or pricing methods used in the market in some way to restart a new escalation cycle, essentially moving to a new price-benefit line. The characteristics and capabilities that will shape the escalation strategy include innovation skills, market power, and market knowledge:

- *Innovation:* The first determinant of which escalation strategy to follow is the level of innovativeness of the company compared with rivals. Companies with high levels of innovation skills can harness escalation within the current primary benefit and also use these skills to generate new primary benefits. Great momentum generators like Apple can continue indefinitely to improve upon the primary benefit that their products offer through technological innovation, the use of new business models, and the reinvention of their value chain. This essentially restarts competition on a new price-benefit line.

- *Market power:* In contrast, to slow, freeze, or reverse the momentum requires a high level of market power over either customers or rivals, as was the case with GE in turbines. Companies that have this power can use it to slow the momentum, but if they don't have this power or cannot create it, they won't be effective in dampening the escalation. Then they need to look to other strategies of pacing the momentum.

- *Market knowledge:* Effective pacing depends on intimate knowledge of the market. Changes in consumers can offer opportunities to create new primary definitions or change the old ones. Shifts to new primary benefits or the use of secondary benefits to neutralize the added advantage that a rival is seeking to make the new primary benefit are difficult to execute. They are determined at the intersection of the company's capability for innovation, the evolving competitive conditions, and changing market demands. The emergence of technology without market interest can be seen in the repeated attempts to launch the AT&T videophone, which was a combination of analog technologies from televisions, cameras and phones. For decades, it was a promising idea. Yet, all the efforts to reach a mass market ultimately failed because, except for videoconferencing, there was little interest. Even after the analog technologies improved and fell in price, consumers still had little interest in answering a videophone first thing in the morning, looking like death warmed over. There simply was not a critical mass of users—no one to call but yourself. However, today the rise of Internet communication, digital cameras, and the widespread use of personal computers has given this idea a new life, as Skype has demonstrated. There are many great ideas whose time has not yet come—and others that are on their way out before we can grasp them. Both of these can be assessed with astute market knowledge.

When faced with escalation, some companies will need to build new capabilities to mount an effective response. If they don't have sufficient innovativeness but need to drive escalation, they need to build their innovation capability. On the other hand, a company that wants to reverse the momentum will have to look for ways to create market power, perhaps through mergers and acquisitions or regulations. Finally, if a company wants to periodically re-seize momentum, it needs to ensure it has the necessary innovation, market-sensing capabilities, and new product launch capabilities. The company's competition and capabilities will shape strategy, but the strategy may also shape capabilities and competitors.

Because the processes of proactively harnessing the momentum or constant reinvention of the primary benefit (and the acquisition of competencies to do so) are exhausting, most firms would prefer to freeze the line in place or reverse the momentum. The company that is dampening or reversing the escalation must have some leverage to do so, such as product-market overlaps that allow it to discipline rivals or lock-ins with customers. Microsoft has been able to do this for many years in software, but it also had to drive escalation at points when the primary benefits were about to change (as with the browser wars). Of course, the success of any approach to reverse or freeze the escalation depends on the strength of this leverage. If the expected price line is elevated too much, firms can expect others to enter the market and begin the escalation again.

Reversing the momentum is only workable under three conditions that enhance a firm's market power:

- There are relatively few competitors that need to be controlled.

- There are high barriers to entry protecting the established firms.

- Firms have the will and ability to scale back capacity to create artificial shortages that inflate prices.

If the industry lacks the conditions for reversing the momentum, then these conditions may be created by restructuring the industry. In industries like cement, a small number of international players are buying up local producers country by country. They then reduce the capacity within each country to create shortages and price increases, and they increase the toehold overlaps among their territories to influence one another's pricing behavior. Because transportation costs are high, there are natural barriers to entry that limit the ability of imports to undermine the price increases they impose on the local market. So prices can be elevated in markets previously fraught with escalating price wars.

MANAGE PERPETUAL MOTION

Managing momentum is more critical in hypercompetitive markets than more stable environments. When imitation is easy, technology is changing quickly, or customer needs and priorities are shifting frequently, the escalation trap can constantly reappear. Firms can be expected to attempt to escape the trap by finding a new primary benefit to replace the old one, thus endlessly restarting the cycle of differentiation and escalation. A new primary benefit can become the key differentiator for products in the market because: (1) it used to be a secondary benefit, but has become first priority for customers because the competition has neutralized the previous primary benefit; or (2) it is a new benefit not previously offered in the market, but suddenly valued by customers because of their changing tastes; or (3) when (some) firms develop production capabilities that make it affordable for the masses. The cycle seems endless.

But as we saw with Primo, companies that can recognize this pattern can harness the momentum of escalation to drive their own progress and derail the strategies of rivals. Or, if they build sufficient market power, they can freeze or reverse the momentum, reducing the escalation by creating a shakeout or a consolidation of the market. And if their people have been trained and motivated with the stamina to resist "initiative fatigue," they can also manage a series of cycles of escalation to re-seize the momentum repeatedly.

No matter which momentum strategy you select, escalation will eventually restart owing to changes in technology, disruptive competitors and entrants, or shifting customer needs. The battles are never won permanently, just transformed. You are always jockeying for better positions. And, as former British Prime Minister Margaret Thatcher once said, "You may have to fight a battle more than once to win it."

FIVE

The Diamond in the Rough

How to Keep Finding Your Best Competitive Position

Much of this book has been about how you can identify the type of commodity trap you are in—and then deploy strategies to beat it. In other words, we have been mostly concerned with how firms can extricate themselves from an existing or fast-approaching commodity trap. But, of course, an ounce of prevention is often worth a pound of cure; anticipation is preferable to apocalypse.

In the future, spotting a commodity trap before it is sprung—and taking preventative action—will be critical. At the same time, it is important to recognize that, for those prepared to seize the day, commoditization brings opportunities as well as threats. Every down has a potential upside. Integral to dealing with commodity traps and exploiting the windows of opportunity they present is the ability to look ahead to see how a market might develop so you can stake out an advantageous position. As the Chinese philosopher Lao Tzu said, "Opportunities multiply as they are seized."

Hardnosed, fact-based analysis can often identify windows of opportunity that are not apparent to others. The key to anticipating a trap lies in understanding what competitors are doing, either by looking at their historical behavior or, as in the Primo case described in chapter 4, trying to understand their strategy based on the trajectory of their moves.

Price-benefit analysis can be used to understand shifts in competitive dynamics and positions, as well as to recognize when the primary benefit may be about to shift. Such shifts are like earthquakes. They can shake up an entire industry—but they can be anticipated. By identifying the fault lines and tremors that could lead to bigger changes, a company can position itself on the right side of the fault line, or even take up a position to take advantage of the quake itself.

By looking at different benefits in more detail and understanding how they are changing over time, we can gain deeper insights into the opportunities that exist to defeat commodity traps, when using the re-seizing, outflanking, selecting, containing, and sidestepping strategies discussed earlier.

Most executives I talk to are comfortable with the notion of seizing opportunities. They understand that a proactive stance is often far better than a reactive one. The problem is that they can't necessarily see the window of opportunity in time to take advantage of it. Anticipating moves in their markets is what many able executives struggle with. Too many feel like deer caught in the headlights, surprised by unforeseen threats.

The questions I hear a lot are: How can we see the earthquake coming? When do we need to make the change? How can we tell what our competitors are going to do before they do it? The answers lie with *anticipation.*

FOOD FOR THOUGHT

To begin to find some answers to these questions, let's look at some research I did in New York.[1] It is a great example of an organization making sure that it anticipated where the market was going and being nimble enough to make the changes to avoid an approaching trap.

I worked with a hotel firm with the goal of helping it reposition the restaurants in its New York City hotels.[2] The firm needed to know which battles it should fight and how it could outflank its rivals in the highly proliferated NYC restaurant market. We quickly got down to the basics. What drives the price of a meal? Is it location? The cuisine? The patron's experience in the restaurant? Are the drivers of prices changing, and what implications does this have for repositioning the menus and pricing structure? Should the company open or close some restaurants, or add entertainment and other features?

We statistically analyzed Zagat's New York City restaurant data for a three-year period by regressing the price of a meal on various restaurant benefits. The restaurants ranged from Gray's Papaya, which featured a $2 two-dogs-and-a-tropical-drink special, to the elegant French-seafood restaurant, Le Bernardin, which set patrons back an average of $75 each for a dinner and a drink. The sample included almost seventeen hundred restaurants, serving all cuisines (including Chinese, Mexican, Russian, and American) in all the city's boroughs and neighborhoods.

The results from our price-benefit analysis for the restaurant's experience and cuisine were fascinating. We found that the restaurant experience and special features added different amounts to the average price of a meal.

The primary benefit, the customer's in-restaurant experience, was based on the sum of three 30-point scales on which customers rated their satisfaction with the restaurant's food, service, and décor, respectively.[3] So experience could be rated from 0 to 90 points in theory, but no restaurant scored either a 0 or a perfect 90. Each point of improvement in the experience rating adds a little over a dollar to the price of a meal, running from approximately $7 to $8 for the lowest customer experience score, to $70 for the highest experience score. We found that satisfaction with the in-restaurant experience explained 73 percent of the variance in prices, while cuisine explained only 3.5 percent of the additional variance in prices, and location only an additional 2.5 percent. In short, a great experience is more important than what kind of cuisine these customers ate.[4]

Other features, such as outdoor or hotel dining, dancing and entertainment, and the other unique attributes were responsible for approximately 1 percent of the variance each. But these features explained 21 percent of the variance in prices. The relative importance of these benefits was a surprise to the hotel management, who expected location to be the most important driver of prices.

Having found that location isn't everything, our next surprise was that, even though locating a restaurant in a hotel added $2 to $3.60 to the price of the meal, the pricing impact of hotel dining had eroded over the previous three years. For the hotel firm's managers, this provided urgency and the rationale for some serious changes and soul-searching. Ultimately, they decided to refurbish some restaurants to look like stand-alone restaurants by moving their primary entrance to the street, with a secondary entrance to the hotel's lobby. This was a way to hedge the decline in the price power of hotel dining.

SOMETHING FISHY

The research led the hotel firm's managers to change tack in a variety of ways to ensure that they seized emerging opportunities. They discovered that live entertainment did not add to the price of the meal because cover charges are not included in most restaurants' meal prices. At the same time, restaurants with dance floors, which were charging $4.50 to $7.25 (with an average of $5.88) more, were increasing their pricing power over the previous three-year period. Clearly the designers of Starwood's W Hotels knew what they were doing when they built nightclubs and restaurants with dancing as part of the format as a way to distinguish the chain.

The hotel firm's management recognized the wisdom of this. Rather than spending money on more outdoor dining, as they had wanted to do before the analysis, they decided to create dance floors— especially when they saw that outdoor dining actually added less to the price of a meal and was declining in pricing power.

The research didn't stop there. What about what's actually on the plate? The type of cuisine clearly has an effect on price. Steakhouses added $5.70 to $7.40 to their tabs, and French restaurants added $3.75 to $5.30, while Chinese and Greek restaurants were actually penalized for their cuisine. Pizza restaurants suffered the worst, knocking off $4.00 to $5.70, and Thai restaurants lost $2.30 to $4.20.

What stood out here was that the pricing power of different cuisines was in flux. While French restaurants were commanding a premium, their pricing was actually eroding. Steakhouse prices were just treading water, while seafood prices were increasing. Greek and Chinese food prices were coming back from the depths (moving from negative to zero), and Russian cuisine prices were booming. In response, the hotel firm added seafood items to several menus, combined Russian and French offerings in some previously French-only restaurants. And some Thai restaurants were closed and replaced with other cuisines, especially seafood, which added $1.40 to $2.70 (with an average $2.05) to the price of a meal, and which was increasing in pricing power.

Clearly, location was still an issue. The pricing power of restaurants in different locations varied. The hotel firm reduced the square footage dedicated to its restaurants in price-depressed areas, assuming that local competition was very tough or the location was too out of the way to become a dining destination for non-guests. The space was converted to other revenue-generating activities.

Finally, we examined the changing impact of the primary benefit (the customer in-restaurant experience) on prices. The expected price line became steeper over the three-year period, indicating that high-end restaurants received a greater price premium for the good customer experience they offered while low-end restaurants were seeing the erosion of pricing power. This happened because incomes were rising in New York City at the time, and people were frequenting upscale restaurants. To hold market share or stimulate growth, low-end restaurants had to offer a better deal, so they lowered prices. For instance, the average price of a meal for the restaurants with the lowest experience ratings fell from $7.20 to $5.80 over the years. This was good news for restaurants in the hotel chain's high-end brands, but it created a dilemma for the middle-position properties.

To make up for price deterioration, the hotel firm decided to improve customer experience and modify cuisines, rather than to reduce prices, in its middle-positioned brands. In its budget hotels, the firm reduced prices to underpriced local rivals in order to generate the traffic needed to be profitable.

Hard analysis plus the willingness to adapt to the findings is the way to anticipate approaching commodity traps and to seize the opportunities on offer. Our New York restaurant research statistically identified the annual price-benefit equations that showed which benefits were important and which were growing in importance; the hotel firm used this information to anticipate what the market was likely to do. In downturn markets as well, this method can be used to anticipate which locations, cuisines, experiences, and other unique restaurant features are declining in value to the customer, so that restaurants can be modified, opened, or closed based on the trends.

TO AFFINITY AND BEYOND

This sort of analysis can also be used to identify hidden opportunities in other market places. It can help identify the right value proposition by benchmarking prices and benefits against competitors within the same segment, and help set R&D priorities so that product development is focused on what customers are willing to pay for—not now but in the future. It has been used by collectors to determine prices for stamps or coins of different national origin, age, condition, and bundled in collections. It has also been used to determine if the brand names, national origin, type, content, or age of fine wines and cigars are shifting in importance.

Perhaps the most prevalent use of this type of price analysis is in real estate markets, where price-benefit analysis is used widely by developers, lenders, property tax assessors, realtors, and bargain hunters. It can help find neighborhoods and properties that offer investment opportunities that others are not yet capitalizing on. Home prices are determined by various benefits, including the quality of the home's neighborhood and a variety of specific features, such as the home's size, decks or porches, number of bathrooms or bedrooms, and other features like fireplaces and amenities. Local governments, insurance companies, and some of the risk-averse mortgage companies impose discipline on the market by using appraisers trained to use statistical data to establish the expected price of a property. This results in a real estate market in which the vast majority of the variance in pricing is explained by the price-benefit equation.[5] So the price-benefit equation is commonly used in the real estate industry to set or assess the price of a new residential property coming to market, as predicted from the analysis of recent sales.

But companies can use price-benefit analysis for much more, such as spotting unrecognized values, or future values, in the housing market. For example, one California real estate developer, Affinity Neighborhoods, uses price-benefit analysis to identify hidden bargains based on what customers are willing to pay for. Affinity uses a proprietary software program to find hidden gems in some of the poorest and least-attractive neighborhoods in California and Arizona based on the changing value of neighborhoods. The program uses sophisticated algorithms to combine detailed information about crime statistics, school test scores, and even weather reports to establish the expected price of being located in a given neighborhood. The company then predicts the erosion or improvement of value of specific areas based on changes in the characteristics of each neighborhood. As a result, Affinity can identify and prioritize the recovering and up-and-coming neighborhoods that can be developed or gentrified based on favorable changes in the factors that are most predictive of neighborhood values. This also identifies neighborhoods that should be avoided or areas where properties should be divested before price erosion occurs.

Affinity Neighborhoods also looks for hidden gems using its price-benefit analysis to create an equation that predicts what the price of a home should be based on the going price per square foot, the number of bedrooms or bathrooms, and the presence of a fireplace, finished basement, or other features. This equation then makes it possible to pinpoint the expected price of a specific house of a particular size or with other value-adding features. Affinity then compares this expected price with actual prices to find the bargains (estimated expected price less the actual prices). So it can identify underpriced homes on the market, often offered by a seller in a hurry.

In addition, price-benefit analysis reveals the exact value of each feature and characteristic by establishing how much of the price difference between properties is associated with their different features. And it tells Affinity how much each feature contributes to the variance in prices among the different properties. The company identifies specific homes where the cost of upgrading or repairing problems (such as adding a deck, upgrading a kitchen, or fixing a roof) is less than the increase in fair market value that would appreciate from those upgrades and repairs. Affinity has been able to spot opportunities to buy, renovate, and resell homes, generating an average return of 50 percent on investment before the 2008/2009 credit crunch.

During downturns in the real estate market, price-benefit analysis is used to identify the neighborhoods that will be least affected by price declines, even identifying which neighborhood characteristics are driving down neighborhood prices most (such as crime rates, average lot size, variety and type of nearby employers, number of other homes for sale, school quality, playground availability, traffic congestion, and centrality to large employers. And as upturns begin to materialize, the price-benefit analysis can identify which house and neighborhood attributes will be the first to recover, providing advance notice of the opportunities to buy low and sell high. In addition, as prices decline, the real value of a house is often not the listed price of the home. Sellers often refuse to lower prices out of stubbornness and denial of real price declines. This allows mortgage buyers or lenders to identify how far a house is under water, given the mortgage it carries. Mortgages are typically listed in the public records (registries for deeds and other property rights). If the real home value falls below the amount of the mortgage, opportunities arise to either change the seller's mind with facts, or to buy up poor-quality loans for sale in the future. In some areas mortgage buyers are identifying the neighborhoods that will recover the most quickly, buying up risky loans in those neighborhoods at 40 percent of the real value of the home, refinancing the loan with the home-owner, and waiting to sell the loan when the real value of the home rises, thereby improving the price of the loan by reducing the risk of the loan with stronger collateral behind it.

While price-benefit equations are less commonly applied in non–real estate markets, they have been used to associate a specific price tag with the benefits of different products, especially in markets where pricing is not transparent to naïve buyers and sellers, such as valuing coins, antiques, and art. This allows collectors and traders to find bargains that can be bought from or resold to those less in the know. Markets implicitly value each benefit offered by a product and factor it into the price, just like stock markets look at company characteristics when valuing their stocks. So clear price-benefit relationships and price-benefit equations emerge in many markets, making arbitrage possible in many cases where prices are not known to all the buyers and sellers.

Collectors use price-benefit equations to find the expected price that cigars, stamps, and coins will probably fetch at auction, or they use the information to find the best deals—commonly private sellers who have grossly underpriced their goods. In addition as the market goes up and down, collectors can monitor the differences in buyer preferences and modify, expand, or contract their collections accordingly. For example, gold coins' prices increased during the recent downturn, while stamp collecting has seen a long-term decline in prices at the low and middle segments, starting well before the downturn began.

SEIZE THE OPPORTUNITY: SET PRODUCT R&D PRIORITIES

"Be prepared," Boy Scouts are advised. Executives facing commodity traps could learn from that mantra. The key to creating effective strategies for beating the commoditization trap is to be prepared by getting your R&D efforts in sync with your future needs for new benefits or lower costs. In particular, you have to create the customer benefits desired in the different segments or markets you wish to enter as part of a containment or outflanking strategy, and you must sequence the benefits being produced by R&D to enable efforts to avoid, undermine, or overwhelm rivals driving commoditization in the market.

As we saw with Apple's iPod, timing the introduction of new features can greatly extend the lifespan of a prestige product. The analysis of price and benefits can help to guide product R&D strategy to prepare it for generating benefits needed to create the value propositions of the future.

But where should a firm's R&D dollars be dedicated?

SKATE TO WHERE THE PUCK WILL BE

New products and services are the source of tremendous growth for companies. Robert Cooper, in his book *Winning at New Products,* estimates that products not sold five years ago (including extensions and improvements) account for an average of 33 percent of company sales, with this figure rising to 100 percent in some fast-moving industries.[6] Yet studies have found that failure rates for newly launched products are as high as 50 percent or more.

Why? In their analysis, Susumu Ogawa and Frank Piller conclude that the primary reason for such failure is that these products "have no market."[7] In other words, they provide benefits that consumers are not willing to pay for. Further, Ogawa and Piller point out that traditional marketing research approaches for assessing customer preferences, such as focus groups and even quantitative research, have serious limitations. The biggest problem is that these tools are based on customers' stated intentions rather than actual purchasing behavior, and the two are often quite different.

Companies can also end up in trouble by launching "me-too" products. Cooper found that superior, differentiated products with real customer benefits have five times the success rate and market share of such products.[8] In other words, companies do far better when they find distinctive positions on the price-benefit map by offering benefits that customers are willing to pay more for, rather than imitating and moving to crowded positions.

My experience with senior managers tells me that even the best managers don't do a very good job at finding these positions. When asked how their products stack up against rivals, they often have divergent views of the value offered by their products. They frequently disagree over the positioning of their own products or deny the benefit of rival products. Despite access to a wealth of data, they often ignore hard facts in favor of opinions and misperceptions, typically relying on their outdated frontline experience and intuition that lacks understanding about the latest customer purchasing behavior and competitor pricing strategies. Product price and benefit data are often locked up in data warehouses or exist only in the minds of a few individuals, waiting to be synthesized, codified, and communicated to all the people working on basic research, engineering, design, selling, advertising, and strategic decisions. Visualizing price-benefit positioning is a serious challenge, but displaying your price-benefit position in a convincing and accurate way can be a powerful tool for envisioning and developing better products and price-benefit positioning strategies that justify premium prices and encourage increased purchases by customers.

Hockey great Wayne Gretzky famously commented that he skates to where the puck is headed. Some of this ability is based on an intuitive grasp of the physics of ice and the movement of other skaters. This intuition might be enhanced through an analytical program that would calculate the muscularity of the other skaters, the force of a slap shot, the speed of the puck, and the condition of the ice. An analyst or physicist might do this well, but they would not necessarily put the puck into the net. This is what a detailed price-benefit analysis can provide. At the end of the day, it still requires a hockey stick in a skilled hand to size up the situation and act quickly.

Commoditization is a rapidly moving game. There is sometimes little time for detailed analysis. A price-benefit map can be sketched out quickly based on informed but impressionistic data or based on only a couple of weeks of rigorous research. In either case, it offers a graphic illustration of where competitors are now and how they are changing over time. But only industry knowledge, competitor analysis, and some informed guesstimation can get to the right answer from any fact-based analysis. As a result, price-benefit analysis, coupled with managerial intuition and up-to-date experience, are always needed to size up the situation, anticipate where the market is headed, and get out in front.

THE PUCK STOPS HERE

The sort of analysis I have described can help you to reassess your product line by looking at the market through the lens of customer types with different needs and priorities. Products can be mapped and remapped using different benefits on the horizontal axis to see how the positioning of the products change. If you know the priorities that different customer types assign to different benefits, then you can rate and map each of your products using the primary benefit prioritized by each customer group.

For example, suppose your focus group research tells you that, when asked about cars, commuters believe that fuel efficiency is most important with a priority score of 50 out of 100, safety 30 out of 100, and comfortable seats 20 out of 100. Plotting price against fuel efficiency gives you a view of the products as seen by that segment, revealing whether you are positioned well for the commuter segment. The same cars might look very different through the eyes of eighteen-year-old male drivers, who value vastly different characteristics, giving engine power and sexy body design considerable more weight than commuters do. Thus the same products will be positioned very differently when plotted on a graph of price versus engine power or body appeal. The results can be used to reposition your product line to fit the segment you want to target or, conversely, to determine the customer segment that would be most attracted to your products and, hence, where you should target your marketing and product R&D efforts.

The fact is, commoditization is not going away soon. Pragmatic executives learn to live with it. Smart executives will use it to their advantage. They will find ways to analyze and anticipate their markets. In this way they will be able to identify windows of opportunity that can be exploited. I have tried in this book to demonstrate how it is possible not just to survive—but to actually thrive—on commoditization.

In sum, by using price-benefit analysis and good managerial judgment to anticipate the different commodity traps and opportunities created by them, executives can stay one step ahead. Or, to put it another way, you avoid what Oscar Wilde described as the extremes of the cynic—"a man who knows the price of everything and the value of nothing"—as well as the pitfalls of the sentimentalist— "a man who sees an absurd value in everything and doesn't know the market price of any single thing."

In the end, though, it is up to you. Anticipate the trap. Escape the trap. Destroy the trap. Turn the trap to your advantage. Or get trapped. It's your choice.

Tips for Doing Price-Benefit Analysis

The method that underpins this book's research is price-benefit analysis, a technique that uses tools and techniques that I have developed over many years. These methods are based on what economists call *hedonic price regression*—a statistical tool to compute a price-benefit equation that predicts which product characteristics drive prices in a given marketplace. Creating price-benefit maps and estimating price-benefit equations with statistical tools requires many judgments and can be done for many purposes. This appendix offers a more detailed exploration of the price-benefit methods and approaches used to illustrate the cases in the main text of the book. Considerable detail and rigor lies behind these analyses. This appendix aims to capture some of the learning gained in doing them.

OVERVIEW: MAPPING THE MARKET

To identify the three commodity traps, I have developed a tool called a price-benefit map. This underpins much of the analysis in this book and was the subject of an article I wrote for *Harvard Business*

Review ("Mapping Your Competitive Position") in November 2007. Movement toward the lower left corner of a price-benefit map (low price, low benefit) indicates deterioration and movement toward the lower right of the map (high benefits and low prices) indicates escalation. Meanwhile movement that converges on a single point (a focal product) on the map surrounds a specified position on the map with many closely positioned products, indicating proliferation.

In its simplest form, a price-benefit map shows the relationship between the primary benefit that a product provides to customers and the prices of all the products in a given market. Positioning maps help companies penetrate the fog that shrouds the competitive landscape. Creating such a map involves three steps:

- *Frame your analysis—Define the purpose of the analysis and the market you want to study:* To draw a meaningful map, you must specify the boundaries of the market in which you are interested. First, identify the consumer needs you wish to understand. It is important to cast a wide net for products and services that satisfy those needs, so you aren't blindsided by fresh entrants, new technologies, or unusual offerings that meet those needs. Second, choose the country or region you wish to study. Finally, decide if you want to tackle the entire market for a product or only a specific segment—do you wish to explore the retail or wholesale market, for instance, and are you going to track individual products or brands? You can create different maps by changing these frames of analysis. The type of map you draw depends on your purpose—that is, are you interested in today's position, in a trajectory over the past to extrapolate the future, or in differences between different segments of the market?

- *Define the dimensions of the map—Choose the price and identify the primary benefit:* Once you've defined the purpose and the market, you need to specify the scope of your analysis of prices. You have to decide here whether to compare initial prices or prices that include life-cycle costs, prices with transaction costs or without them, and the prices of unbundled or bundled offers. These choices depend on the yardsticks that customers use in making purchasing decisions. Be sure to use inflation-adjusted prices because you can be fooled into thinking prices are rising when they are in fact falling in real terms. The next step is to identify the primary benefit—the benefit that explains the largest amount of price variance.

This can be complicated. A product typically offers several benefits: basic functions, additional features, durability, serviceability, aesthetics, ease of use, and so on. Companies often differentiate their offerings by focusing on a different benefit to their rivals. But the success of strategies depends on the value that customers, not companies, place on features. To determine that value you must draw up a list of benefits offered by all the different products or brands in the market and then gather data on how customers perceive those benefits. You should try to use unbiased data, rather than rely on gut instinct or top managers' opinions—and the primary benefit can be found through focus groups or hard statistical analysis using regression analysis of price against the benefits to see which has the most influence on price. There is a growing array of product ratings produced by independent organizations and publications such as *Consumer Reports* and JDPower that can be used for this analysis. Sometimes the primary benefit is actually a combination of linked features. So for example, my analysis showed that "customer experience"—a combination of three highly correlated attributes of restaurants (décor, quality of food, and service)—accounted for 73 percent of the price variation of New York City restaurants.

- *Interpret the data—Plot positions, draw the expected price line, find strategic groups and trends, and determine the implications of the results:* Once you have identified the primary benefit, you are ready to draw the map by plotting the position of every company's product or brand in the marketplace according to its price and level of primary benefit. Such positioning maps show the relative positions of competitors on a common scale. Next, you must draw the expected price line—the line that best fits the points on the map. The line shows how much customers expect to pay on average to get different levels of the primary benefit. In addition, the slope of the line tells us how much more a customer is likely to pay for a higher level of the primary benefit. Products lie on either side of the line not by accident but because of the companies' strategies. Firms position a product above the line to maximize profits, which they can do by simply raising the price in the short run or by enticing customers to pay a higher price for secondary benefits. Alternatively, companies can slot their product below the line to maximize market share by simply charging less than expected or dropping some secondary benefits to attract price-sensitive customers. Sometimes, products fall below the line because they contain "detractors"—characteristics that repulse or dissatisfy customers. Finally, you can look for products that cluster into groups of similar products. Some clusters will contain the low-end, basic products, others the mid-range, premium, or superpremium products. The clusters may fall all along the line, or may reflect pricey (above the line) or discount (below the line) positions. If the analysis is done at several points in time, trends may be revealed, including how the expected price line is changing over time, how products are being repositioned, which product benefits are gaining or losing importance as drivers of pricing in the market, and whether a cluster is becoming more competitively intense with new entrants and growing or big hit products.

More details salient to these three steps follow.

FRAMING YOUR ANALYSIS

Without a specified purpose or definition of the market to be studied, price-benefit mapping and analysis can become a time sink.

Define the Purpose of the Price-Benefit Analysis

The possible uses for price-benefit mapping and equations are many and varied. But it is important to determine what specific strategic issues you wish to answer before you begin your analysis: Anticipation or diagnosis of the trap? Outflanking proliferators? Undermining low-end discounters? And so on. Otherwise, it is easy to get bogged down in confusion. It is also helpful to determine what strategic actions you are willing to consider. What levers are under your control that can or should be used to deal with the issues you are analyzing? Are you looking to make changes in your R&D or advertising budget? Your product positioning? Your cost structure? Your pricing decisions? Do you want to see the trends over time or look at the current position of rivals? Clarity about the purpose of the analysis can save a lot of time and money in data collection and reduce confusion about how to use and interpret the data. The purpose affects how you will define market boundaries of your analysis, select the methods used, and do the interpretation of the results, as discussed in more detail below. That being said, sometimes a lack of clarity is beneficial. It can lead to the serendipitous discovery of issues and opportunities that could not have been anticipated earlier in the process. So it is sometimes good to let the data speak for itself, rather than putting on too many blinders.

Determine the Boundaries of the Market

When applying price-benefit mapping to a market, interpretation can be difficult if the map is not constructed properly. First and foremost, it is important to define the market's boundaries by limiting the geographic scope and customer segment being analyzed. Where there are important differences in products, customers, or competitors that would confuse the interpretation of the map, lumping them together may blur how customers are defining the primary benefit offered in the market or the method they use to define pricing in the market. So getting a tight market definition is important.

If you are seeking to get a picture of how widely different segments are competing with each other, the analysis will be improved if it includes all rival products (and even substitutes) that vie for the same or similar customer needs. Otherwise, the map may give an incomplete view of the market. Typically a wider field of products and competitors is better for avoiding getting blindsided by new entrants, unusual products, substitute products (especially if they serve the same customer need or purpose), or when some rival firms are not on your radar screen. It is sometimes useful to treat a group of products with similar prices and primary benefit levels as a single product if they are individually not important but collectively make up a significant part of the market or if they could potentially change the future primary benefit. This prevents ignoring seemingly unimportant threats.

Finally, when a wide definition of the market has been chosen because of the way the data have been collected, that data may aggregate many product-customers segments. For example, analysis may be done separately for small, medium, large, sports, and luxury sedans, as well as minivans, SUVs, and pick up trucks. Or the analysis may be done for the automotive industry as a whole. Interpretation of wider market data must be based on the understanding that the definitions of price and primary benefit will be aggregated or averaged across the market. While it is harder to figure out what is driving prices at the individual product-customer segment level, aggregated data can be used to establish information about competitors' positioning and pricing strategies across groups, capturing the cross segment competition. This exposes the market's aggregate definition of primary benefit, the positioning of strategic groups of competition within the industry and the average pricing behavior across all the included segments. Thus it can provide information for the corporation as the whole and suggest what the firm might do when preparing for several segments by identifying commonalities across the segments and establishing priorities for the level of resources that should be allocated to R&D of various benefits.

DETERMINING THE DIMENSIONS OF THE PRICE-BENEFIT MAP

The next step in creating a price-benefit map is to determine the way customers and competitors define pricing and the primary benefit offered in the market, so that the two dimensions of the price-benefit map can be established. The primary definition of price is determined by how buyers calculate or perceive price during their purchasing decision. Customers may look only at the initial purchase price, or they may look at the total cost of ownership, the price including hidden costs such as the time to learn how to use the product or to search for the product, and the price after delivery and service or finance charges. Depending on the market definition selected for the analysis, the price may be the price to wholesalers, end users, or others in the distribution chain.

It is also important to use inflation-adjusted prices during times of high inflation to avoid misinterpretations. On the basis of nominal prices, the market may look like it is moving toward the upper left of the price-benefit map. However, when inflation is removed, the market may be moving in the opposite direction. This is especially problematic when prices are rising owing to input costs. Whether the costs created by shortages in raw materials (including metals, labor, or energy costs) are passed on to customers, it must be considered whether the price increases completely or partially recover the rising input costs for the manufacturer.

In addition, the definition of price should fit the product-customer segment selected for analysis. In the case of coal, pricing might be viewed as the material cost of the coal itself, the material costs plus delivery charges, or the material and delivery costs plus the cost of removing sulfur or ash content. Market segments with sophisticated buyers, like utility companies, consider the full cost of usage. However, the residential segment may be less discerning and rely on material cost prices plus delivery only.

The primary benefit is the benefit that is the most significant driver of price differences. It is determined by starting with a list of all the benefits offered by products within the boundaries of the industry selected for study, including durability, defect rate, consistency, safety, efficiency, serviceability, sturdiness, comfort, workmanship, power, performance, reliability, satisfaction with the experience, features, accessories, energy usage, ease of use, conformance with standards, aesthetic appeal, size and weight, or any other attribute or characteristic that may have value to the customers within the segment chosen for analysis.

Then regression analysis is used to estimate a price-benefit equation that best fits the data. This method determines the best linear formula for:

$$Price = f \text{ (Benefit A, Benefit B, etc.)}$$

The equation with the highest overall R^2 will determine what definition of price and primary benefit should be used as dimensions of the map. (R^2 is the amount of variance in prices—the dependent variable—that is explained by all the independent variables in the regression equation—product benefits, including performance, attributes, features, and other product characteristics of value to customers.) The incremental R^2 associated with each benefit tells how much each benefit contributes to the variance in prices—with the largest incremental R^2 indicating which benefit is the primary one.

Benefits are typically measured by surveying customer perceptions of each benefit, such as the satisfaction with a restaurant experience. However, more quantitative measures of a product's actual benefit can be used when customer perceptions closely reflect the real benefits of the product. It is important to avoid use of *management's* perceptions of product benefits to avoid biased maps.

Even a so-called commodity product such as coal can present unexpected richness in potential benefits. For example, the benefits of coal include its BTUs per ton, sulfur content, hardness, ash produced, and the quality of its supplier (reliability of shipment and consistency of product quality).[1] Since most buyers are looking for the energy content of the coal, BTUs per ton is the primary benefit offered in the market. However, secondary benefits, such as sulfur content and ash, may become the most important if users become more environmentally conscious owing to regulation or public pressure. In times of shortages, users such as electric utilities become more concerned with supply disruption than BTU, ash, or sulfur content. Then they are willing to pay extra for reliable delivery. Typically, secondary benefits affect the overall price of a product, but to a lesser degree than the primary benefit. However, depending on changes in circumstances, a secondary benefit may become the new primary benefit, as the old primary benefit erodes. As a result, the price-benefit map may have to be drawn with different dimensions for different time periods.

A less rigorous way to determine the primary benefit is to ask customers in focus groups, but this does not actually look at their purchasing behavior, only what they are saying they will do. Focus groups are also not good at determining the aggregate purchasing behavior of the market, which is the average of all the customers in the market, including those who may not be in a focus group study. While extensive customer surveys can reveal the "average customer," they are often expensive and take too long to execute, which can be a serious drawback in rapid-change environments. So it is better to look at actual purchasing behavior—using the prices customers actually paid for the product and the benefits that they actually got when they bought the product.

More Methods for Measuring Benefits

Data about product benefits is readily available from many sources such as the Internet, trade associations, consumer magazines, data warehouses, the sales force, government agencies, *Consumer Reports*, product-testing laboratories, consumer-rating organizations, wholesalers, distributors, or competitive and business intelligence firms. It is important to remember that different types of data create different types of interpretation biases. Nothing is perfect. Price and benefit data may be based on managerial impressions, hard measures of a product's benefits (such as warranty data or crash tests for cars), focus group ratings, survey data on the mass perceptions of users of the firm's products, or surveys of all potential users. Managerial impressions are fast and cheap, but can be very biased. Hard data is often readily available, but customer perceptions may not match them. Focus groups measure the ratings of people who have tried the product, but the masses may not be aware of the product's various features and attributes. Surveys of the firm's customers are often biased by not including the purchasers of rival products and don't consider nonusers and potential users. Surveys of all potential users are costly and often provide data too late for timely decision making or are biased by the fact that nonusers and potential users don't know what the products are capable of.

Because the number of benefits that might be included in the price-benefit equation is so numerous, it is typically better to combine benefits that are highly correlated in order to simplify the analysis and avoid problems that can occur when doing the regression analysis. In cars, the primary benefit identified in our research (except for sports cars) turned out to be the composite of a car's carrying capacity (passengers, fuel, and luggage space), engine power, fuel usage, and crashworthiness, all variables that tend to be correlated. In general, larger cars tend to have more powerful engines, be less fuel-efficient, and suffer less damage in a crash than smaller ones. Hence they tend to cost more than small ones, all else being equal. Because these four aspects of cars are all correlated, they can be combined into one overall measure, labeled *platform*. Note that each of the variables is measured using different units of measure (such as miles per gallon, crash damage ratings, number of passengers, etc.). In such cases, it is important to remember to use statistical *standardization*—which removes the units of analysis by converting each variable into standard deviations from the mean—so that the diverse variables can be added together.

Composite measures of benefit can be created based on one's market intuition, but it is better to use more sophisticated statistical means. Composite measures can be discovered using statistical tools commonly employed by market researchers, such as principal components analysis and factor analysis. Available in most statistical packages, such as SPSS and SAS, these statistical methods identify the benefits that are so correlated that they belong together on one scale.

In addition to correlated benefits, compound benefits can be created through a score or index (similar to a credit score) that combines several uncorrelated, but equally important benefits. In cell phones, the primary driver of prices is their advanced functionality. This is a count of the number of advanced functions that a cell phone has (i.e., the functionality of smart phones and PDAs, such as calendars, e-mail, Internet browsers, high-resolution cameras, and videogames). They are not correlated, but they add up to a more useful phone, for which people are willing to pay more.

In pharmaceuticals, safety (side effects) and efficacy are not correlated in many cases. A drug's efficacy may be high despite its potential side effects, or vice versa. Yet, efficacy and safety may be equally important because they act like substitutes for each other or customers may even require both to be present. Many consumers won't take a drug unless it both works and is safe. Other patients consider the trade-off between efficacy and safety, with some deciding an efficacious drug is worth the pain of adverse side effects, while others may prefer to take a less efficacious drug because the risks of side effects are so low as to be worth the gamble in trying a drug with questionable impact. Although uncorrelated, safety and efficacy could be combined into a compound score to represent the primary benefit in the industry because most patients will evaluate these together, and they can't be separated from each other during the purchasing decision because one cancels out the other.

Interpretation of the data is greatly affected by the type of data used. For example, if you use hard data to measure reliability of cars and you find people won't pay a premium for reliability, it may be because reliability is no longer a differentiator or that customers can't identify cars that are truly more reliable so they won't pay a premium for this benefit. Or they may be working from old information, remembering that some manufacturers sold an unreliable product when they made their last purchase. So purchase behavior may not be directly related to hard measures of benefits. Nevertheless, when purchases are big-ticket items, purchased and used frequently, or highly important or salient to customers, most markets are "efficient." In other words, people know the real value of the product's benefits from their experience and from information gathered from the Internet, consumer guides, and product raters. The bigger the ticket, the more importance to the buyer, and the more used the product, the more knowledgeable the buyer, the more customer perceptions reflect the realities of the market.

Many sources of data are often available, sometimes with conflicting information, so it is important to validate whatever data are used. If the hard data or customer rankings conflict with managerial impressions, managers often ignore the hard data or discredit the conclusions. Thus, it is important to get managerial buy-in for the selected definitions, sources, and measures of benefits and prices before the price-benefit map and equation are presented for discussion. Otherwise the decision-making process can get deadlocked by those who refuse to accept the results due to denial, or the decision-making process may be derailed by those who choose to play politics with the data to enhance their personal goals and power.

INTERPRETING THE DATA

A price-benefit map is easy to misinterpret if the map is drawn improperly or if the user lacks sophisticated knowledge of the industry's context needed to understand the nuances of competition.

Draw the Price-Benefit Map and Expected Price Line

With price and the primary benefit determined, the price-benefit map is built by plotting the price against the primary benefit on a graph. Because this price-benefit map is based only on the primary benefit in an industry, it does not entirely explain differences in prices, which could also be explained by secondary benefits that were significant in the price-benefit equation estimated by regression analysis. However, a price-benefit map based on the primary benefit simplifies the view and shows relative positions of competitors based on a common scale. As discussed previously, deviations from the expected price line are commonly explained by secondary benefits, strategic choices to milk a product (by pricing above the line), strategic choices to build market share (by pricing below the line), strategic decisions to tilt the line to cause one end of the line or the other to lose market share, or omitted secondary benefits or other omitted variables (such as intentionally induced shortages, difficult-to-measure intangibles including image, or the strength of distribution channels for which no data has been collected).

Price-benefit mapping can be used to create knowledge at the company, brand, product line, or product levels of analysis. At the most simple unit of analysis, a price-benefit graph can show the positions of products within a marketplace. However, such maps can be confusing if there are too many products on the map, making the complexity of the map beyond comprehension. So groups of products can be considered as a company's integrated product line, requiring the price-benefit map to use ellipses that cover the area that each company's product line occupies. This allows one to study how the product lines overlap and compete for strongholds on the price-benefit map. It can also be used to observe the pattern of competitive pressure that groups of firms apply to each other's product line. One can also graph the price and benefit offered by different brands in a market to assess the brand positioning strategies being pursued by competitors. A brand's rating of its price and benefit position can be created by taking the average across all products with the same brand, and the average might be weighted by how many units are sold of each product within the brand, to give the big sellers more emphasis in the measuring a brand's attributes. One can even graph the positions of entire companies by plotting the weighted average of the benefits offered and prices charged for each company's set of products within the product market being studied. Graphing companies, product lines, or brands can reduce the complexity of a price-benefit map, simplifying the picture to make it easier to interpret, but eliminating some of the richness shown in maps based on detailed product positions. The use of brand- and company-level weighted-average data is advisable only when the company's product portfolio is relatively homogeneous. When the portfolio is very heterogeneous, product graphs are more accurate and revealing. However, product-based price-benefit maps can be confusing if there are too many products, so if the firm sells a wide range of products, it might be better to calculate and plot the benefit positioning of its different brands, rather than its individual products or the company's average.

Based on the primary benefit and the unit of analysis, an "expected price line" is then drawn for the market. The "expected price line," in its simplest form, embodies the notion that "you get what you pay for" or, more accurately, that "you pay for what you get." Thus, the line is typically positively sloped. In exceptional cases, a negative line can exist if lower benefit–higher priced legacy products remain on the market owing to switching costs, customer loyalty or inertia, or lack of market transparencies concerning prices and benefits. Generally, such negatively sloped lines disappear as the market matures, and these problems go away. Curved lines are also possible, but typically the curved part of the line is at the extremes. A low price may continue at a steady rate until a threshold level of primary benefit exits, and then the price line takes off. Or the price may reach a ceiling level, no matter how much extra benefit is added. Again, in the long term, these floors and ceilings generally disappear as the market figures out that excessively low- or high-benefit products don't pay off.

When there is too little data to do a formal statistical analysis, the expected price line can be drawn by visual inspection of all the points on the price-benefit map to find the line that runs through the middle of all the points on the map—with half the points above and half below the line. The best approach is to determine the line by more formal statistical means using a price-benefit equation to get the linear equation that best fits the price-benefit data. This technique is known as regression analysis. The slope of the expected price line is the coefficient associated with the primary benefit from the price-benefit equation, and the intercept of the expected price line is the intercept from that equation as well.

To get the best estimate of the price-benefit equation, it is wise to weight each product on the price-benefit map by its volume sales in units or dollars—a technique commonly found in statistical packages. This methodology prevents small sellers from distorting the line you are estimating.

Figure A-1 represents products by circles of different sizes proportionate to the products' sales volume. Ignoring the circle sizes

FIGURE A-1

Estimating the expected price line weighting the impact of sales volume

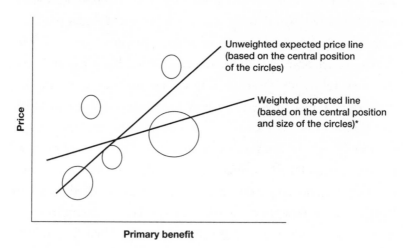

*Circle sizes are proportional to sales volume of each product.

and drawing the expected price line based only on points at the center of the circles produces the unweighted line. If we weigh the larger circles more, we get the weighted line. In this hypothetical case, the general implication is that if we weigh in the consumers' purchasing behavior (volume purchased), we find that we get an expected price line with a flatter slope. This means that products of increasing primary benefit are not earning the price increases that we would expect purely from looking at how companies priced their products. Weighting the products by sales volume is a good way to be sure the results reflect the observed behavior of purchasers.

With the expected price line drawn, it is possible to see how individual products fall along the line. As discussed previously, products along the line can be grouped and labeled as ultra-low, basic, midrange, premium, super-premium, or ultra-premium value propositions. In addition to positions on the line, some "pricey" positions above the line may exist when secondary benefits add to the price of the product, or owing to milking strategies in which firms intentionally charge high prices to generate margins at the expense of market share. In other cases, a premium above the expected price line may be paid because of shortages for that particular product or because of intangible assets not used in the price-benefit equation (e.g., brand image). Some bargain (or discount) positions below the line may be created for strategic purposes such as buying market share. Or they may exist because the products have detractors that reduce their price or because the secondary benefits they offer are missing or below average.

Finally, a deeper analysis can be created by estimating the expected price lines and price-benefit equations for the products of each major competitor separately, as I did for hotel firms in chapter 3. This gives details about how the firms are setting their pricing strategies differently. And may give hints about how and why different firms can elevate their expected price lines above others. Expected price lines and price-benefit equations can also be estimated for each product or customer segment separately to show how different subsets of the market are seeing the market, and to clarify the different critical successful factors for the different subsets of the market.

Understanding the Price-Benefit Map

If products are positioned at different points in time based on their changing prices and primary benefit levels, it is possible to see their trajectory, determine their rate of movement, assess the possible strategic intent of rivals, and project the landscape of the future map if the movement continues unimpeded. And the price-benefit map can be used to determine the relative attractiveness of different positions on the map in the future or to find unoccupied positions on the map being ignored by firms. Thus, the map can be used to answer or discuss several questions, such as:

- What are the opportunities and threats that are apparent based on the competitive intensity of various value propositions? How will players move in and out of the various value positions?

- Why are rivals moving in the trajectories and at the rates they are? What opportunities and threats are created by their movement?

- Is the market commoditizing? Which pattern is it following (movement to the lower left or right corners? Is the space around your position filling up with aggressive rivals?) What does this mean about your future?

- What are the threats to your major products (the 20 percent that make up 80 percent of your sales)? Are they being surrounded, driven down toward the ultimate value point or the low priced–low benefit corners of the price-benefit map?

- Where are the weaknesses in your product line or brand positioning?

- How is the price-benefit equation changing? Based on this analysis, where do you think the expected price line will move in the future? Will a new primary benefit emerge in the market? How soon? Why are these changes occurring?

- Challenge the assumptions you use in sketching out a future map. You can ask: "What if" you changed the assumptions? Suppose the rivals change trajectories or rates of speed in the movement on the map? What would the landscape of the future look like? What should you do differently if your "what-if" analysis assumptions turn out to be right?

- How can you proactively change the map of the future to create a more favorable future?

Clearly, one cannot interpret a price-benefit map and changes in it without understanding the driving forces behind the map. New value positions on the map may appear, disappear, or change position because of underlying forces, such as changing technology, the entry or merger of rivals, the reinvention of business models, and shifting customer tastes or demographics. The expected price line may change position, and volatility in secondary benefits may occur because of these forces. And the competitive intensity may escalate as competitors move positions because of these forces as well, making interpretation of the data difficult. So industry knowledge is critical to interpretation of the maps.

Two pieces of industry knowledge are particularly critical to understanding the financial implications of shifts in the expected price line: price elasticity and capacity constraints or inflexibility. The *price elasticity* of demand indicates whether and how much consumption of a product or service goes up when prices are reduced. More elasticity means that demand is highly affected by prices. If demand is inelastic, a tilt in the line or an elevation toward the upper left corner of the price-benefit map will not have much effect on consumption of the product. Price elasticity and capacity constraints often interact.

Consider the Primo case in chapter 4, when the slope of the expected price line became flatter (as illustrated in figures 4-2 to 4-4), the demand for the high end increased, and the demand for the low end decreased. The high end's prices declined relative to the low end—that is, the value offered by the high end increased (i.e., its benefit-to-price ratio increased) and the low end's value decreased despite its price decline. Demand switched to the products offering the greater value (i.e., the higher benefit-to-price ratio), rather than to the lowest-priced goods.

Compare this with the case of the restaurants described in chapter 5. When the demand went up for high-end restaurants in New York because of rising incomes at the end of the 1990s, the restaurants raised prices to reduce their value (decrease their value-to-price ratio) and ultimately decreased demand for the high end. Meanwhile, in Primo, lower prices at the high end led to higher value (higher benefit-to-price ratio compared with the low end) and increased demand. But in the restaurant case, higher demand resulted in higher prices in the high-end restaurants. In sum, is higher demand associated with higher or lower prices or vice versa?

The difference in the two cases was created by different causal orders and the restaurants' constrained or inflexible capacity. *Causal order* means the direction of causality—rising demand was caused by factors other than price changes for the New York restaurants. Demand changes then affected price, not the other way around. In addition, when the demand went up for high-end restaurants, the restaurants were unable to increase capacity to meet the demand. Waiting lines increased, and customers were turned away. Lack of space and fire laws prevented them from adding more seats. So to maximize profits, they raised prices. This cut the waiting lines, and reduced the demand to fit the capacity available. Primo had no such constraints, and raised capacity to meet the demand increase at the high end that it stimulated via offering a better value.

In brief, we have two cases of tilting expected price lines—one gets steeper over time and the other flattens over time—with contradictory effects on the higher end. In one case (Primo) the high end achieved lower margins but higher growth in demand, while in the other case (restaurants) the high end had higher margins and an eventual decrease in demand. The difference was due to price elasticity, fixed capacity, and causal factors unrelated to prices. Clearly, industry knowledge is critical to interpretation and understanding.

In general, there are at least six important factors to consider when looking at the impact of a tilt in the line:

- *Price and benefit elasticity:* How much does market share respond to price declines at either end of the line, or improved benefits at either end of the line? Is the market sensitive to these changes or is demand fixed? The price and benefit sensitivity will determine which part of the line gains share.

- *Capacity constraint:* Can the market increase supply when demand goes up, or will it raise prices to cut the demand, waiting lines, or backlog to fit what it can produce? If capacity is inflexible or lumpy, then short-run reactions will include price increased to constrain demand and maximize profits.

- *Exogenous shifts in demand:* Is something other than price or benefits changing the customers' willingness to pay, such as increased disposable incomes, a credit crunch, new customer demographics, or changing tastes? These could change the demand for different segments on the price-benefit map. So the price or benefit impact on growth of one end of the line or the other may be swamped by these macro changes.

- *Technological change and competition:* Are these factors changing the slope of the expected price line? Why? Is competition or technology making the primary benefit obsolete, or a necessity to play? If so, then lowering prices or raising the primary benefit may have no effect on demand.

- *Price and benefit ceilings and floors:* Are their limits to what customers will pay or benefits that they are willing to buy? Tilts that move the line outside these floors and ceilings may not have any effect on demand or may even have opposite effects (e.g., when prices signal a fire sale or when products are overengineered).

- *The source of cross-segment competition:* A line can flatten because the low end raised prices or the high end lowered them. And a line can become steeper because the low end reduced prices or the high end raised them. Each change implies that something different may be occurring, such as rising input costs being passed through at one end or the other of the line for various reasons. For example, the reasons may include price insensitivity at the high end, coupled with having no choice to pass costs through at the low end because of the price sensitivity of low-end customers.

It is important for interpretation purposes to use your industry and customer knowledge to supplement the observed changes on a price-benefit map, and to challenge your unstated assumptions and conventional wisdom within the market to make interpretation of price-benefit analysis more useful. This includes analyzing the impact of substitute products.

Plan Your Offensive

Once the analysis is complete, the next step is to evaluate possible moves and countermoves. Here, again, it is important to understand where you are on the map and the relative strength of competitors.

Do you have the initiative? Price-benefit mapping can be used to assess your aggressiveness against different competitors by looking at the vulnerability of a rival's products. After identifying the 20 percent of products that are generating 80 percent of the revenues of each important rival, you can ask several questions: How aggressively are your products positioned around those products? Can you set a commodity trap for them? Which key rivals' major products are most vulnerable to attack, given how other players are targeting those products? Could reducing the price of your products inflict more pain on a competitor's key products than on your firm (such as when Southwest reduced prices on key routes and the higher-market-share major airlines were forced to follow—at great losses to them)? Should the firm position additional products against the competition's major products in order to hold them in check or to weaken them? Or are other players already doing that for you? Can the competition's major products be outflanked by products with more or less primary benefit? Or can they be undermined with lower price or a different combination of benefits that yield the same total level of primary benefit? Have you chosen the right competitor to attack?

In addition, you can determine if you have the initiative or are too reactive. Cargill, the producer of food, agricultural, and risk management products and services, did a study looking at the price and benefit moves made by the firm and its rivals in several agricultural markets. Its managers asked: How often do we move first or are we just responsive? Are our reactions to moves by rivals slower or faster than other rivals? How many major price-benefit changes have occurred over each five year interval during the last twenty years? Are we laggards or leaders in these changes? Is there a pattern to how rivals respond to us?

After considering these questions, Cargill decided that it was too slow and too unresponsive in some markets, even though it was proactive and leading in others. And it discovered that the frequency of major price-benefit moves was increasing over time. When the board saw the facts, they recognized that Cargill did not have the capability to move fast enough in the future, given the current rate of acceleration in moves that redefined quality or price in the marketplace. So the firm reorganized its entire structure, processes, and incentives to enhance its speed and agility to capture the new opportunities. Internal venture capital boards were created, many P&L subunits were restructured into key building blocks that could be assembled or reassemble as needed to compete for the rapidly changing market.

Asking these questions, among others, will allow the firm to make clearer and more explicit plans about beating carefully selective rivals, because you can't target everyone everywhere all the time—you must pick you battles and fight them smartly.

GETTING THE MOST OUT OF YOUR PRICE-BENEFIT ANALYSIS

While the price-benefit map, price-benefit equation, and other tools add clarity and precision to the analysis of commoditization, seeing and countering commoditization is only partly science. There is also an art to anticipation. Each set of complex price-benefit maps can be interpreted in different ways, requiring solid judgment. Identifying the types of commoditization revealed by these maps and deciding how to react through anticipation is the essence of vision and leadership. The maps and analysis aid vision, as telescopes and microscopes reveal distant and tiny facts, or as radar and night vision goggles allow us to see in the dark. Without them we are flying blind. But what is seen and the reaction still depends in large part on who is wearing them.

Price-benefit analysts can get carried away, doing analysis for the sake of analysis because it is so "elegant." So you must actively take steps to get the most out of your price-benefit mapping and avoid analysis paralysis. The best way to avoid this problem is to define the scope of your analysis carefully, as discussed above. Price-benefit analysis is an art form, requiring many judgments. Knowing your purpose and frame is not enough—the goal is to avoid garbage-in, garbage-out, and to get actionable conclusions.

NOTES

Chapter 1

1. Interview with Steve Heyer, Tuck School of Business, Hanover, NH, February 21, 2006.

2. Thanks to Alberto de Cardenas, Paul Kim, Joep Knija, Mark Potter, and Aaron Smith; as well as Sameer Nadkarni, Jim Sole, and Igor Popov for their analysis of Harley-Davidson as of 2002.

3. Price-benefit analysis involves graphing the position of all products in a marketplace using each product's price against its *primary benefit*—the most important product benefit that drives pricing in the market. Then it includes using statistical analysis to identify the *expected price line*—the line that predicts the average price for a given level of the primary benefit. Products positioned above (or below) the line include price premiums (or discounts) for secondary benefits offered (omitted) by the product, good (or bad) brand image, and intentional strategies to milk the product by charging an unexpectedly high price above the line at the risk of losing market share (or to buy market share by charging an unexpectedly low price below the line for the product). See Richard A. D'Aveni, "Mapping Your Competitive Position," *Harvard Business Review*, November 2007, 110–120, for more details on the price-benefit analyses used in this book.

4. Thanks to Carolyn Ball, Dora Fang, Nao Inoue, Lee Johnson, and Eric Young for their analysis of the motorcycle industry in 2004.

5. Clifford Krauss, "Women, Hear Them Roar," *New York Times*, July 25, 2007.

6. "H-D and Buell Support Female Riders," www.motorcycle.com, December 24, 2008.

7. Harley-Davidson, *Annual Report* 2007.

8. John Wyckoff, "How Harley-Davidson Lost Its Cool," *Marketing Trends*, October 11, 2004.

9. The Walmart effect is the impact of a large firm offering everyday low prices through continuous cost cutting and economies of scale, forcing rivals to continually follow with more price cuts until the entire market is trapped in a downward spiral. We have seen this effect in the airline industry, where Southwest Air has used cost cutting to drive all the majors into a similar strategy.

Chapter 2

1. Thanks to Gianmario Verona at Bocconi University in Milan, as well as Bernhard Termühlen, Chad Miller, Michelle Coyle, Mariana Garavaglia, Cynthia Landrebe, and Julien Bonneville for their research on the fashion industry.

2. It is worth remembering that Zara is positioned higher in the U. S. market due to the higher cost of shipping from its central warehouse in Europe to the United States and to the greater costs of overhead associated with running its small number of U.S. stores. In Europe, it is in a discount position that is transforming the industry.

3. Michael Silverstein and Neil Fiske, *Trading Up* (New York: Portfolio, The Penguin Group, 2003).

4. Robert J. Frank, Jeffrey P. George, and Laxman Narasimhan, "When Your Competitor Delivers More for Less," *McKinsey Quarterly* (Spring 2006), www.mckinseyquarterly.com/article.

5. Ibid.

6. Evan West, "Spicing up the Gum Trade," *Fast Company*, October 2007, 71.

7. Thanks to Alice Tsui for her research on outsourcing and automation.

8. Thanks to Amol Pinge for research on automation in the auto repair industry.

9. http://www.bloggingstocks.com/2007/03/16/kroger-to-wal-mart-bring-it-on/

10. "Kroger Fact Book," www.thekrogerco.com.

11. Thanks to Alexander P. Hennessy for his research on the software industry.

Chapter 3

1. "Rapid Rise of the Host with the Most," *Time*, June 12, 1972.

2. See Andrew Nelson, "The Holiday Inn Sign," *Salon*, http://dir.salon.com/story/ent/masterpiece/2002/04/29/holiday_inn/index.html.

3. I used the company's self-rating unless it led to inconsistencies that didn't match up with what other companies said about their equivalent chains.

4. Thanks to Alexander Hennessy and Ann Schiff for their analysis of the hotel industry.

5. Roger Yu, "Limited-Service Hotels Take On Upscale Ambience," *USA Today*, April 17, 2007, http://www.usatoday.com/travel/news/2007-04-17-limited-service-usat_N.

6. Interview with Steve Heyer, Tuck School of Business, Hanover, NH, February 21, 2006.

7. "How Andy Cosslett Restyled IHG," *BusinessWeek*, May 21, 2007, http://www.businessweek.com/bwdaily/dnflash/content/may2007/db2007 0521_843548_page_3.htm.

8. David Kiley, "Holiday Inn's $1 Billion Revamp," *BusinessWeek*, October 26, 2007.

9. "IHG Launches $1bn Holiday Inn Revamp," *The Times*, October 25, 2007, http://business.timesonline.co.uk/tol/business/industry_sectors/leisure/article2733718.ece.

10. See http://business.timesonline.co.uk/tol/business/industry_sectors/leisure/article2733718.ece for a comparison of the old and new signs.

11. Kiley, "Holiday Inn's $1 Billion Revamp."

12. Thanks to Kevin Daniels, Lynette Darkoch, Phil Drapeau, Brian Safyan, Nik Shah, and Jesse Sherman for their research on the casino industry.

13. "Hotel Innovator Ian Schrager and Marriott International to Create Next-Generation Lifestyle Boutique Concept," Marriott press release, June 14, 2007.

Chapter 4

1. Thanks to Francis Barel, Dan Bernard, Craig della Penna, Edwin Lau, Tammy Le, and Darren Perry for their research on the sweetener industry.

2. While the details of the case are mostly accurate, the market, company names, and details have been disguised at the request of the company.

3. By observing the rate of decline in the current primary benefit's incremental R^2 and by looking at the rate of increase in the incremental R^2's of secondary benefits, managers can predict when significant shifts in the main basis of competition—the primary benefit offered—will occur.

4. Moore's law: The power (speed of processing) of microprocessors doubles every eighteen months.

5. Kathleen M. Eisenhardt and Shona L. Brown, "Time Pacing: Competing in Markets That Won't Stand Still," *Harvard Business Review*, March–April 1998, 59–69.

6. Interview with Ken Burns at the Tuck School of Business, Hanover, NH, October 9, 2007.

7. Interview with Steve Loranger, February 7, 2006, in Hanover, New Hampshire.

8. Thanks to Angus Boyd, Scott Hazard, Florian Jaeger, Theodore Nickolov, and Brendan Warn for their research assistance on the iPod market.

Chapter 5

1. This research is featured in my article "Mapping Your Competitive Position," *Harvard Business Review*, November 2007, 110–120.

2. Thanks to Deepa Poduval, Alinia Asmundson, Edmund Poku, Arun Mathias, and James Lau for data collection, cleaning, input, and analysis tools related to the restaurant industry.

3. These three items were combined into one scale because they were highly correlated with each other.

4. Variance explained was determined by looking at the incremental R^2's associated with each feature or attribute of the restaurant generated by regression analysis. We regressed the average price of a meal (including one drink) on the restaurant's features and attributes to see which had the biggest effect on prices.

5. The price-benefit equation is the equation yielded by a regression analysis of prices paid against the products benefits. In residential real estate this would be the price paid in recent house sales versus the house's neighborhood, square footage, condition, number of bedrooms and baths, and special features such as gardens, pools, decks, fireplaces, etc. The equation identifies a coefficient for each house feature or attribute that estimates how much each affects the price of a house. And it allows sellers to estimate the price of a house given its particular features and attributes.

6. Robert G. Cooper, *Winning at New Products: Accelerating the Process from Ideas to Launch*, 3rd edition (Cambridge, MA: Perseus Books, 2001), 4.

7. Susumu Ogawa and Frank T. Piller, "Reducing the Risks of New Product Development," *Sloan Management Review* 47, no. 2 (Winter 2006): 65–71.

8. Cooper, *Winning at New Products*, 60.

Appendix

1. *BTU*: British thermal units per pound. One BTU is the amount of heat required to raise the temperature of one pound of water 1 degree Fahrenheit.

Acknowledgments

1. McKinsey & Co., for example, adopted and published a refined version of the price and benefit mapping tools I first developed in chapter 1 of *Hypercompetition*. See Ralf Leszinski and Michael V. Marn, "Setting Value, Not Price," *McKinsey Quarterly* (1997) 99–115, for a discussion of how McKinsey & Co. has advanced and used my tools in their consulting engagements. Cargill did a highly creative multi-million dollar study of the magnitude, frequency, and initiation of moves and counter-moves using tools developed originally in *Hypercompetition* for the price-quality arena. Cargill's analysis looked at two of its major lines of business, resulting in a major reorganization of the company to cope with the rapidity and aggressiveness of the maneuvering they observed. This study looked at Cargill and its competitors to see who sought advantage in the price-benefit arena, including who initiated the moves and who responded in which arena, as well as to determine how fast the responses were, how frequent the moves were, and how bold or revolutionary the moves were. This led Cargill to reconsider its strategy and organization, after realizing that the acceleration of the moves were outpacing the firm's ability to compete, leaving Cargill in a responsive mode in the lines of business studied. In addition, after extensive training on price-benefit mapping and analysis, Nolan Norton & Co. sold numerous consulting jobs using the principles of *Hypercompetition*, developing advanced and unique consulting methods that moved my thinking forward in many ways.

ACKNOWLEDGMENTS

To look more closely at the dilemmas created by common commodity traps, I embarked on a systematic study of price erosion and product-benefit competition that involved many research assistants. In addition, over the recent years, I have learned a great deal from the many others whom I trained to use the price-benefit mapping tools I describe in this book. Companies, including AGFA, Cadbury Schweppes, Deloitte Consulting, Deutsche Bank, General Motors' Luxury Car Division, Learning Systems Milan, Monsanto, PepsiCo International, Philip Morris, and Philips Electronics have used my models in their strategic planning and decision making processes. (*Note*: No proprietary data from any of my clients have been used in this book without their approval. Otherwise, all information comes from publicly available sources, interviews with nonclient executives, or other private sources.)

I also have learned from those who have advanced my work on price and benefit competition to create applications beyond what I envisioned when I first invented them, such as McKinsey & Company, Cargill, and Nolan, Norton & Co., a division of KPMG Europe in Amsterdam.[1] Other collaborations have been very fruitful as well. Led by Meredith Ceh, a former student of mine, Wilson Learning Corporation—the second-largest training company in the world—developed early methods for price-benefit mapping. Spending over a half million dollars developing ways to systematize, simplify, teach, and use these mapping methods, Wilson Learning made many contributions to the price-benefit analysis methods described in this book. The Wilson Learning team and/or I have used these approaches with clients such as GE Capital, British American Tobacco, Rockwell International, US West, and Colgate-Palmolive, among others. Since the time I regained the rights to these Wilson Learning methods and materials, I have trained a generation of Tuck students and research assistants to use price-benefit mapping and to find the price-benefit equation for various industries. Over fifty of them have done research that inspired many of the examples used in this book. These projects are cited with their permission and thanks throughout the book. I owe a debt of gratitude to all my students and research assistants who have contributed to my knowledge, as I hope I have contributed to theirs. It has been a great blessing to have such great students and assistants to keep me young of mind and spirit.

I would like to thank several people who contributed greatly to this book. First and foremost, I am deeply indebted to Robert Gunther. Through serious illness and considerable personal sacrifice, he stuck with me. His dedicated work on this book was both a reflection of his great intellect and outstanding integrity, as well as the close friendship we share. His research efforts, insights, editing, and many substantive contributions to the structure, writing, and theory of this book were so crucial that this book would not exist without them.

Des Dearlove and Stuart Crainer of Suntop Media in the United Kingdom have also made considerable contributions to the framing and clarity of this book. Their editorial and writing skills have made this book more accessible to many more readers, so they deserve considerable thanks as well.

Melinda Adams Merino and Astrid Sandoval of the Harvard Business Press, as well as Anand Raman of *Harvard Business Review*, were also instrumental in helping me to frame the book, providing guidance and focus that made it much more readable and well thought out. They pushed until I got a product that stood the test of their scrutiny, helping me to fix logical inconsistencies and thematic flow. The book would not be half as good without their guidance.

Many staff and faculty members at Dartmouth College were very supportive of this project. Several colleagues have been very helpful in the formulation of my thinking on the topics in this book. They have helped me at formal seminars and in our hallway discussions. They include Koen Pauwels, who has worked with me on academic articles derived from this book, and Constance Helfat, who first suggested that I look at the hedonic price regression literature and opened my eyes to the possibilities that it might hold. Sydney Finkelstein, Vijay Govindarajan, Margie Peteraf, Victor Stango, Ken G. Smith, Gianmario Verona, and others have all shared ideas with me freely, and I thank them greatly. I also appreciate all the efforts of my administrative and academic coordinators, Dale Abramson, Sheryl Berberick, Marcia Diefendorf, Heather Gere, and Donna McMahon, as well as the librarians at Feldberg Library, including Sarah Buckingham, Karen Sluzenski, and Jim Fries. I thank them for their help. Ted Hartnell deserves special thanks for his work on graphics.

Of course, I must mention by name the research assistants and students who have been credited and thanked in footnotes all through out the book, including: Anuraag Agarwal, Alinia Asmundson, Paul Auffermann, Carolyn Ball, Francis Barel, Dan Bernard, Julien Bonneville, Angus Boyd, Alberto de Carenas, Tak Wai Chung, Tim Clark, Michelle Coyle, Kevin Daniels, Lynette Darkoch, Tim Delfausse, Craig della Penta, Shambavi Desgupta, Phil Drapeau, Justin Engelland, Dora Fang, Mariana Garavaglia, Mathew Goldfine, Richard Haas, Saad Hasan, Scott Hazard, Alex Hennessey, David Hoverman, Nao Inoue, Florian Jaeger, Suneth Jayawardhane, Lee Johnson, Scott Kendall, Paul Kim, Joep Knijn, Cynthia Landrebe, Edwin Lau, James Lau, Tammy Le, Anandam Mamidipudi, Arun Mathias, Ryan Meyers, Chad Miller, Mike Murray, Pat Murray, Sameer Nadkarni, Prasad

Narasimhan, Theodore Nicklov, Creighton Oyler, Minkyu Park, Darren Perry, Amol Pinge, Deepa Poduval, Edmund Poku, Igor Popov, Mark Potter, Brian Safyan, Ann Schiff, Darryl Seet, Nik Shah, Douglas Sharp, Jesse Sherman, Cem Sibay, Aaron Smith, Jim Sole, Bernhard Termühlen, Alice Tsui, Michael Wang, Brendan Warn, Navam Welihine, Geoff Wilson, and Eric Young.

I want to reiterate my gratitude to all of them for their kindness in sharing their thoughts and research efforts with me. Their contributions to individual cases and analyses were so voluminous that they are too varied to enumerate here. However, they are much appreciated.

Several executives were very influential in shaping my thinking about commodity traps, differentiation strategy, and competitive repositioning. While I have quoted only a few of them, I thank all of them for sharing how they are dealing with their commodity traps, including: Elyse Benson Allan (president and CEO, GE Canada), Jim Bailey (president and COO, US Trust), Doug Baker (CEO, Ecolab), Roger Ballou (CEO, CDI Engineering), Jim Bouchard (CEO, Esmark/Wheeling Pittsburg), Ken Burnes (CEO, Cabot Corporation), August Busch IV (CEO, Anheuser-Busch Companies), David Calhoun (vice chairman, General Electric), Mike Dan (CEO, Brinks), Marijn Dekker (CEO, ThermoFisher Scientific), Dave Dillon (CEO, The Kroger Company), Peter Dolan (CEO, Bristol-Myers Squibb), Fred Eppinger (CEO, Hanover Insurance Group), John Faraci (CEO, International Paper), Fred Festa (CEO, WR Grace & Company), E. V. (Rick) Goings (CEO, Tupperware), Richard Goldstein (CEO, International Flavors & Fragrances, Inc.), Hugh Grant (CEO, Monsanto), Bill Harrison (chairman, JPMorgan Chase), Fred Hassan (CEO, Schering-Plough), Jim Haymaker (SVP, Strategic Planning and New Business Development, Cargill), Ernesto Heinzelmann (director and president, Embraco), Steve Heyer (CEO, Starwood Hotels and Resorts), Peter Hoffman (president, Grooming Products, The Gillette Company), Susan Ivey (CEO, Reynolds

American), Mike Jackson (CEO, AutoNation), Bill Johnson (CEO, H.J. Heinz Company), Mike Johnston (CEO, Visteon), Mike Jordan (CEO, EDS), Steve Loranger (CEO, ITT Industries), Terry Lundgren (CEO, Federated Department Stores), Frank MacInnis (CEO, EMCOR), Bernie Marcus (founder, Home Depot), Reuben Mark (CEO, Colgate-Palmolive), Tom McInerney (CEO, ING US Financial Services), Peter Murphy (senior EVP and chief strategic officer, and special assistant to the CEO, The Walt Disney Company), Ron Nelson (CEO, AvisBudget), Morgan Nields (chairman and CEO, Fischer Imaging Corporation), Jack Novia (managing director, Americas Region and SVP, Customer Solutions Group, Hewlett-Packard), Steve Odland (CEO, Office Depot), Rod O'Neal (CEO, Delphi), Gary Rodkin (CEO, ConAgra), Frank Russomanno (CEO, Imation), Tom Ryan (CEO, CVS Caremark), Ed Schneider (Chairman, Triton Holdings, LTD), John Shiely (CEO, Briggs & Stratton), Adrian Slywotzky (vice president, Oliver Wyman Consulting), Alex Smith (CEO, Pier 1 Imports), Mooryati Soedibyo (president director, Mustika Ratu Consumer Products Corporation, and vice chairman of the Indonesian Parliament), Tim Solso (CEO, Cummins Engine Company), David Spears (CEO, Illinois Tool Works), John Stropki (CEO, Lincoln Electric Company), John Surma (CEO, US Steel), Jim Tobin (CEO, Boston Scientific), John Tyson (CEO, Tyson Foods), Peter Volanakis (President and COO, Corning), Bob Walter (founder and chairman, Cardinal Health), Mike Wedge (CEO, BJ's Wholesale Club), Wendell Weeks (chairman and CEO, Corning, Richard Wolford (CEO, Del Monte), and Ed Zander (CEO, Motorola). I thank them all for their generosity, for sharing their thoughts and insights, for filling me in on their companies, for granting permission to use their quotes, and for giving their time to the Tuck School and/or to me. Their help was invaluable.

A special thank you goes to Tuck School dean Paul Danos and senior associate dean Bob Hansen, who continued financial support for this project over several years. I appreciate their faith in me, especially since they had to trust that such a long-term effort would pay off someday, in what must have looked like a long shot when I began. Thank you both for sticking with me.

Finally, I want to give my warmest thanks to my family, including my wife, Veronika; my daughters, Gina, Katia, and Tanya; my son, Ross; and my mother and father, Marion and Anthony D'Aveni. They gave me the motivation and support to write this book, as well as the love needed to live my life. I don't know what I would do without them.

INDEX

ABOUT THE AUTHOR

Richard A. D'Aveni is Professor of Strategic Management at the Tuck School of Business at Dartmouth College. He holds a PhD from Columbia University and received his undergraduate degree from Cornell University; he is also an inactive attorney and CPA. He was listed among the Thinkers 50 in 2007 and 2009, a listing of the world's top management thinkers published by the London *Times*, *CNN.com*, and the *Times of India*. In addition, he was named one of the seven most influential strategic theorists in the world by the Corporate Executive Board. D'Aveni has received many other awards for his work, including the prestigious A.T. Kearney Award, and was named a Fellow of the World Economic Forum in Davos, Switzerland. He has published four books prior to *Beating the Commodity Trap*, including the international bestseller *Hypercompetition*, which coined the phrase, and has published articles in *Harvard Business Review*, *MIT/Sloan Management Review*, the *Financial Times*, and the *Wall Street Journal*, as well as in several top academic journals. D'Aveni has been the private sounding board and adviser to several *Fortune* 500 CEOs, the presidents of two G-7 countries, and numerous other CEOs in Europe and the United States. He has worked with numerous *Forbes* 100 wealthiest families in India, Indonesia, Italy, Korea, Mexico, Russia, Turkey, and the United States. One of his major interests is helping others to start English-speaking MBA or executive programs overseas, in places such as India, Israel, Mexico, Japan, and Vietnam. D'Aveni enjoys his two homes, one in the mountains of New Hampshire, and the other in a renovated 1830s palace in the historic center of St. Petersburg, Russia, only blocks away from the Hermitage.